DONDE COMEN DOS, COMEN TRES

WHEN YOU CAN
FEED TWO,
YOU CAN CERTAINLY
FEED THREE

FIESTAS

TIDBITS, MARGARITAS & MORE

FIESTAS

TIDBITS, MARGARITAS & MORE

MARCELA VALLADOLID

PHOTOGRAPHY BY
Isabella Martinez-Funcke

HOUGHTON MIFFLIN HARCOURT • BOSTON • NEW YORK • 2019

For information about permission to reproduce selections from this book,
write to trade.permissions@hmhco.com or to Permissions, Houghton Mifflin
Harcourt Publishing Company, 3 Park Avenue, 19th Floor, New York, New
York 10016.

hmhbooks.com

Library of Congress Cataloging-in-Publication Data
Names: Valladolid, Marcela, author.
Title: Fiestas at Casa Marcela : 75 Mexican-style cocktails and appetizers /
Marcela Valladolid ; photography by Isabella Martinez-Funcke.
Description: Boston : Houghton Mifflin Harcourt, 2019. | Includes index. |
Identifiers: LCCN 2018043603 (print) | LCCN 2018044777 (ebook) | ISBN
9781328567536 (ebook) | ISBN 9781328567550 (paper over board)
Subjects: LCSH: Cooking, Mexican. | Appetizers—Mexico. | Cocktails—
Mexico. | Desserts—Mexico.
Classification: LCC TX716.M4 (ebook) | LCC TX716.M4 V3 2019 (print) | DDC
641.5972—dc23
LC record available at https://lccn.loc.gov/2018043603

Printed in China
TOP 10 9 8 7 6 5 4 3 2 1

To Philip, my partner in love, life, work,
and entertaining . . . I love you almost as much as
I love your pasta sauce. Almost!

CONTENTS

HERE'S THE GOD'S HONEST TRUTH: My fiancé, Philip, and I have thrown so many parties we could now do it with three kids hanging from our legs, one hand tied behind our backs, and a glass of wine in the other—all with zero help. (Okay, maybe we'd each need both of our hands.) I set everything up, then we both get to work in the kitchen and clean up together afterward. But guess who does most of the cooking? Philip does! So my biggest thank-you is to him. Without his support and companionship, I would never be so inspired to always open up our home to friends and family. *Gracias*, Felipe. You, me, a bottle of red, and some Luis Miguel on the speakers, gearing up for a party . . . that, to me, is the perfect Friday night.

acknowledgments

To our children, Fausto, David, Anna Carina, and Kongo: Seeing your faces at the table and spending time together are the highlights of these gatherings. Even our fancy dinner parties ALWAYS involve the children, not just ours, but also our guests'. Everyone wins in this situation, and I wouldn't have it any other way.

To everyone on my team at home who loves my children like family: Maria Guadalupe, Luis, Lety, Norma y Lulu, *gracias por todo.*

These are the key folks when I entertain at home. But for this book, I relied on some of my favorite people, who also happen to be incredibly talented.

Isabella Martinez-Funcke: To be completely frank, one of my greatest satisfactions in doing this book together was having you shoot it. Your first book! The first of many for us, I hope! @isabellamfuncke

Vivi Ley: Oh, how I miss you! Thank you for keeping us all on schedule and me from losing my mind. @vivianaley

Hannah Canvasser: It was a pleasure having you bring these recipes to life so beautifully. @farmtomytable

Perla Laborin: For your assistance in the kitchen and overall great attitude towards life, gracias. @perlaflj

Carlos Sanchez, ChezNug, Suge Night, Chestnut, Chester, Chespirito: Anna loves you more than life, and so do I, for your calm demeanor, insight, and fabulous camera assistance. @cheznug

Ernesto Casillas: My love, thank you for always making my face look its very best! @ernestocasillas

Edna: For the cut, color, and style—this is the happiest my hair has ever been! *Gracias!* @ednarmz_hair_mua

Erika Funcke: Thank you for your impeccable style. @hijadetumadredecor

Susan Choung: For your wonderful editing. @suddenly_susan

Jamie Carr: My literary agent at WME. @jamiecarr

Justin Schwartz: My editor at Houghton Mifflin, thank you! @justcooknyc

And to the wonderful companies and artists who lent us your gorgeous tableware, I truly hope you enjoy the photos as much as we enjoyed playing with all your beautiful pieces.

Gary from Collins and Coupe: For your impeccable vintage glassware. @collinsandcoupe

Hostess Haven: For your amazing tabletop rentals. @hostesshaven

Vero at Object Mexico: For all those exquisite Mexican-made items. @object.mx

Linea Norte: For your eco-friendly *and* Mexican-made furniture and tableware. @lineanorte

Fernanda Uribe from Punto Verde Ceramics: For your magnificent creations. @puntoverdeceramics

I'm at my very happiest when the table is set, the music is on, the wine is uncorked, and the smell of dinner is wafting from the kitchen. These moments that I spend with my loved ones are magical, and nothing satisfies my soul more than inspiring others to create their own special moments. *Gracias! Besos!*

—*Marcela*

introduction

When it comes to hosting a party, there are two kinds of people in this world: those who light up like a firefly at the prospect, and those who curl up into the fetal position at the very thought. As you probably guessed, I'm in the first group. But I have to confess . . . I didn't always love playing the host. As a perfectionist, if things weren't absolutely right, I'd spiral into deep despair. *What if the menu is unbalanced? Or the flowers start to wilt?* And God forbid I burned a tortilla chip! Everything had to be just so—to the point that I'd forgo the opportunity to break bread with friends and family because I couldn't handle potential disappointment. That. Was. Me.

My issues are too complicated to delve into here. After all, this is supposed to be a light-hearted book about margaritas (AND SO MUCH MORE)! But basically, as I got older, I cared less about what people thought, which helped conquer my fear of possible imperfections. My focus now is simply on corralling the people I love and feeding them. Don't get me wrong. If you follow me online, you know that I live for details. Days—sometimes weeks—in advance of an event, I go into hyper-list-making mode. I obsess over the menu and text my fiancé, Philip, daily about what food to serve. I create a timeline for every little moment, from getting flowers to doing my hair. I even color-coordinate the outfits for my entire family. (Yes, I do this. Don't judge me.)

When your end goal is to create memories for the people you care about, party planning becomes interesting and fun. It's actually liberating. When I arrived at this point, I finally found the mental space to relax and unwind. They say you get a sense of peace when you create while connected to the source. That's what hosting a party means to me. Too deep, I know, sorry. You just want delicious appetizers and tantalizing drinks. We'll get there in a minute, I promise!

But before we tackle the recipes, I want to put you on the right party-planning path with my best tips for stress-free hosting. This is the real deal—the food and drinks I serve to my guests; how I set the table, pick the plates, napkins, and flowers . . . The most important thing that needs to be said, though, is that if you enjoy the process and do it with the sole intention of bringing joy to your guests, TRUST ME, it will all turn out swell. And that's actually my very first tip . . .

SET THE TONE FOR YOUR GATHERING. If you are nervous, rushed, anxious, annoyed, or just want everyone to go home so you can Netflix by yourself with the leftover wine, then your guests will vibe off that. Set the mood for YOURSELF even before the party starts. Music is on 24/7 over here at Casa Marcela, and the drinks are flowing way before the guests arrive.

THINK ABOUT YOUR GUEST LIST. Who cares about rules and who you HAVE to invite? Do whatever is best so people can enjoy themselves. If that means "forgetting" to invite the party pooper, then so be it. I think I'm speaking directly to my Mexican peeps here, because the question I get asked the most by my own friends and family is how to politely leave people out. Ha!

CREATE A TIMELINE. More than a schedule, a timeline gives you a good idea of what happens next. (Schedules imply a set time to do things, which can lead to forced meals and kill the natural flow of events.) You have to let the night (or day) guide you. When the appetizers are dwindling and the conversation is starting to die out, gently guide your guests to the dining

room. Don't clear the dessert plates until everybody is good and done. Turn up the music when you've gone through a couple of bottles of wine. If mariachi is going to happen (which we have even in the smallest of dinners, because we just do), YOU HAVE TO WAIT until everybody is totally relaxed and, if possible, a little tipsy. Otherwise they won't sing along. (Okay, maybe that tip was a little too specific, but you get the idea. The point is to go with the flow . . .)

PICK A THEME. I don't mean like *The Smurfs* or *Day of the Dead* (although I've done both of these parties, with great success). I mean choose a general idea to rally your event around so your decision-making will be easier. The theme could be a flower, "metallic," shabby chic, seaside, Asian, seasonal . . . anything, really. I've thrown a party inspired by something as random as the colors of a peony. For another party, I made a sushi cake (see page 125) and I had a blast dreaming up a minimalist, geometric black-and-white tablescape, decorated with leaves I stole from my neighbor's bamboo plant. Having a specific theme will help focus you when it comes time to plan your menu, décor, and even what to wear.

GO WITH WHAT YOU KNOW. If that means testing recipes in advance, then get cooking! You want to set yourself up for success and be confident that your dish will be 100 percent delicious. As for the presentation, I'll let you in on a little secret: The glorious photos you see in cookbooks and magazines are orchestrated by a team of pros. None of them are in heels, about to open up their homes for a special event. They rent props and have all sorts of tricks up their sleeves, like staging the bar with fake ice or brushing the food with oil to make it shinier. Odds are, your finished dish won't be a replica of what's in the photo, but knowing that the recipe works is more important. Then, if you have time to play food stylist, knock yourself out.

WRITE OUT YOUR MENU! This is something I really take my time with so I have a good overview of what I'm serving. For smaller parties of four to six, I usually do one appetizer and maybe some cheese and honey. For larger gatherings, up to twenty-four or so people, I offer a selection of three or

four appetizers. I try to have a balance of vegetarian and non-veg dishes. To figure out how much food to make, I usually count on two bites per person for each dish.

FOCUS ON THE TABLEWARE. If you're not a trained chef and you don't have tweezers in your kitchen drawer (you know, to arrange petals on your flan ::*eye roll*::), then your platters, glasses, and utensils can make your food pop. That doesn't mean you have to go out and raid your nearest Williams-Sonoma. You probably have items right in your house that can fulfill a new purpose. That flea-market pitcher could hold fresh-cut flowers and become a magnificent centerpiece. Those shot glasses you bought in Mexico? Serve soup in them! And pluck some big leaves off the tree outside to line your appetizer trays. (Wash them first, though.) Peep at the photos throughout this book and you'll see unexpected uses for regular

household items. I did end up borrowing some beautiful props (check the Acknowledgments for the full list) but for the most part, I did for this book what I do for my parties: walk around the house and hijack items to put on my table. I've also gone "shopping" at my mom's house, which is almost better than rummaging through a vintage store. This way I can mix and match items for an eclectic and visually interesting table.

SERVE FOOD FAMILY-STYLE. That's how we do it at Casa Marcela, no matter how formal the event is. Who's got time for individual plating? I'd much rather park large platters in the center of the table and spend more time with my guests. Then everybody can dig in (after snapping their Instagram pics, of course). It's less fuss for the host but also fosters a more communal dining experience. People can make small talk around the table as they reach for another Chipotle Deviled Egg (page 115).

CREATE A HOUSE DRINK. For a large gathering, concocting a fun, fruity punch with just the right amount of sweetness is less stressful, easier on the wallet, and a surefire crowd-pleaser. That said, I ALWAYS have good wine and a good tequila in the bar for sipping. No matter what your poison is, always, always, always make sure you have enough alcohol. When the booze is kaput, so is the party.

PREP AS MUCH AS YOU CAN IN ADVANCE. I've been known to set the table three days before a meal and then just wipe the plates clean the day of the event. Pick out your platters and serving utensils as soon as the menu is set. Arrange your flowers up to a day ahead. Cook as much as you can the day (or days) before. You'll be so relieved you did when it's T-minus zero till the party starts.

HIRE A SERVER. I know, this may be a little controversial. It's a thing I totally inherited from my dad. If it's within your budget, having a server to help out can be a lifesaver. Maybe not for a dinner for four, but for anything with more than eight guests, I would certainly recommend it. I'm not talking about poaching a server from the best Michelin-starred restaurant in town. Where I'm from, tons of teens are super eager to earn some pizza-and-movie money. Even when I serve family-style, I want the extra set of hands to help set up and fetch whatever we need from the kitchen—be it ice, more water, dressing, bread, or pickled jalapeños! Just have them come early, show them the ropes, and ask them to do the cleanup. Hey, for an extra $20, they might even watch the kiddos while you unwind with an after-dinner drink. #WorthIt

INVITE KIDS TO THE TABLE. If I had to choose between hiring a server or a babysitter (because of the budget), I would ALWAYS pick the server. That leaves the little ones hanging, but it also means they have to join you at the table. I am constantly asked why my children are good eaters, and I honestly believe it's because they're an integral part of all our celebrations. They're seated with the adults and treated like adults and, for the most part, act like adults. (This is why children in Europe are so well-mannered—because they're a PART of the meal, not in exile or zoned out on devices.) Even when I hire someone, the kids help set and clear the table, and serve food, too. Basically, once Philip and I sit down, we let our children and the server handle everything else so we don't have to get up a million times. Trust me, your legs will thank you!

PLAY MUSIC. It needs to be on, it needs to be good, and it needs to be at the right volume. Not so loud that you can't hear one another (unless it's that point in the night when you don't want to actually hear anything BUT the music and the ice clinking in your drink). And loud enough to avoid uncomfortable silences. The party should always feel alive. Remember that music is your substitute host when you have to run from your front door into your kitchen.

CREATE THE RIGHT LIGHTING. I prefer dim lights—candles, if they're an option. Nothing is worse than walking into a dinner in your sexy dress and heels and finding that the room is lit like the school cafeteria. Even if it's an informal gathering (we have those, too!), keep the light low so it's flattering for everyone. Your guests will love you for it.

LAST AND CERTAINLY NOT LEAST, ENJOY YOURSELF! It might not be good for business to say this, but you should feel free to ignore all the tips you just read if it means you'll dive right in and just host however you darn well please. No rules. Just go for it. I can almost guarantee that will be your best party ever.

That's it. That's all I have. I see every event, formal or informal, as an opportunity to create memories with my friends, family, kids...really, anyone who breaks bread with us at our table. My dad always said, "*Donde comen dos, comen tres*," which roughly translates to, "When you can feed two, you can certainly feed three," and that's the motto here. If only I could tell you how many times I had to break out a zip-top bag of frozen tomato sauce (your savior—see page 109) and quickly boil a box of pasta because our party of four suddenly doubled...I should also mention that I'm incredibly lucky to have Philip, who enjoys entertaining as much as I do and is a true partner. He's the real reason things stay on track around these here parts. Philip loves to both cook and clean—and I thank sweet Mexican baby Jesus every day because of it. But I know that's rare, so just focus on the other stuff. I promise that's enough to pull together a really awesome party. Plus, you know where to find me if it's not. So put down this book, slap on some lip gloss, turn on the oven, and chill the rosé. It's fiesta time...

uno: DRINKS

COCONUT MEZCALITAS
(COCONUT MEZCAL COCKTAILS)

SERVES 4

Honey, for rimming

Unsweetened shredded coconut, for rimming

1 cup ice cubes

½ cup mezcal or tequila blanco

2 cups unsweetened full-fat coconut milk (shake the can well before measuring to redistribute any separated cream)

3 tablespoons simple syrup (see Note)

Edible flowers, for garnish (optional)

I have a confession: I can't drink mezcal straight. It's too strong for me. And unless you were born south of the border and grew up with it, it's probably too strong for you, too. Mixing in creamy, sweet coconut milk is a great way to enjoy the spirit without masking its earthy, smoky flavor. And let's talk about the rim on the glasses here. When you sip the drink and get a little bite of the shredded coconut, that's when the magic happens! You can certainly use tequila instead of mezcal, if that's what you usually have hanging at the bar.

Place the honey in a shallow bowl. Place the coconut on a small plate. Dip the rim of a margarita glass or mason jar in the honey to coat, then in the coconut. Wiggle the glass to cover the wet part of the rim completely. Repeat to rim three additional glasses or jars.

Combine the ice, mezcal, coconut milk, and simple syrup in a blender. Process until smooth. Divide the drink among the rimmed glasses, garnish with the flowers, and enjoy!

note

For the simple syrup, combine 1 cup granulated sugar and 1 cup water in a small saucepan. Bring to a boil over medium-high heat. Reduce the heat to low and simmer until the sugar has dissolved completely, about 3 minutes. Remove from the heat and let cool. The syrup can be refrigerated in a glass jar for up to 1 month. Makes about 1½ cups.

ORANGE-CINNAMON SOURS

SERVES 6

2 cups freshly squeezed orange juice (from 4 to 8 oranges)

1 cup tequila blanco

2 large egg whites (from the freshest eggs possible)

¼ cup agave nectar

2 teaspoons ground cinnamon, plus more for garnish

1 teaspoon grated fresh ginger

Ice

6 (2-inch) strips orange zest (peeled with a vegetable peeler), for garnish

6 cinnamon sticks, for garnish

If you ask me, orange, not lime, is the best citrus for tequila. Here I combine that pairing with egg whites to create a drink that's like an Orange Julius for grown-ups. The egg whites give the drink a rich creaminess and make it delightfully frothy. Plus, any time you shake cocktails with egg whites, it gives you instant "mixologist" cred.

Combine the orange juice, tequila, egg whites, agave nectar, cinnamon, and ginger in a pitcher. Stir well to combine. Fill a cocktail shaker with ice, add one-third of the orange-tequila mixture, and shake for 6 to 8 minutes. Strain into two coupe glasses. Repeat for the remaining four drinks. Garnish each drink with a strip of orange zest, a cinnamon stick, and a pinch of ground cinnamon and serve.

MEXICAN TEQUILA and TONICS

SERVES 2

1 small Persian cucumber, shaved into 4 long ribbons with a peeler (see Note)

8 ice cubes

½ cup Don Julio 70 tequila añejo claro or tequila blanco

1 cup tonic water, chilled

2 teaspoons whole black peppercorns

2 lime wedges

2 sprigs fresh rosemary

Think of this as a gin and tonic but with more oomph. The tequila takes center stage, while the peppercorns and fresh rosemary make the drink refreshingly crisp. I love this cocktail with Don Julio 70, a super flavorful tequila añejo that's crystal clear (unlike most aged tequilas, which are darker). If that's not available, use a good tequila blanco instead.

Wrap 2 of the cucumber ribbons around the inside of a collins glass, starting from the bottom and slowly turning the glass to spiral the ribbons upward. Carefully add 4 ice cubes, ¼ cup of the tequila, ½ cup of the tonic water, 1 teaspoon of the peppercorns, 1 lime wedge, and 1 rosemary sprig. Gently stir to combine, taking care to leave the cucumber ribbons intact and in place. Repeat in a second collins glass and serve immediately.

note

For an extra-fancy garnish, shave two additional ribbons from the cucumber. Roll up each ribbon and thread onto a wooden skewer with the lime wedge. Add a skewer to each glass.

TAMARIND-BASIL MOJITOS

SERVES 4

Chamoy hot sauce, for rimming

½ cup Tajín seasoning, for rimming

4 tablespoons granulated sugar

½ cup tequila reposado

1 (11.3-ounce) can tamarind nectar, chilled

½ cup freshly squeezed lime juice (from about 5 limes)

4 lime slices, for garnish

10 fresh basil leaves, plus more for garnish

Ice

Tamarind *agua fresca* was a staple beverage in my fridge growing up, so the chore of peeling, soaking, and seeding fresh tamarind is an everyday thing for me. I won't make you go through the trouble of prepping fresh tamarind—Jumex makes an incredible nectar that's excellent in drinks. You can find it on Amazon or even in some supermarkets. A flavor that goes beautifully with tamarind is *chamoy*, a fruit-based hot sauce that's tangy, sweet, and spicy all at once. I love it on the rim of this drink but also drizzled on tortilla chips or sliced cukes. The other essential part of the rim is Tajín, a seasoning powder of ground chiles, salt, and lime zest that's available at Mexican markets. If you can't find it, make your own from scratch with cayenne pepper, salt, and lime zest.

Pour a layer of chamoy into a shallow bowl. Combine the Tajín and 2 tablespoons of the sugar on a small plate. Dip the rim of a collins glass in the chamoy to coat, then in the Tajín-sugar mix. Wiggle the glass to cover the wet part of the rim completely. Repeat to rim three additional glasses.

Combine the tequila, tamarind nectar, and lime juice in a pitcher. Stir well to combine.

Muddle 5 of the basil leaves and 1 tablespoon of the sugar in a cocktail shaker. Add half the tamarind-tequila mixture and fill the shaker with ice. Shake well and divide the mojito between two of the rimmed glasses. Repeat with the remaining basil, sugar, and tamarind-tequila mixture to make two more drinks. Garnish the drinks with lime slices, basil leaves, and enjoy!

CLASSIC MICHELADAS with CLAMATO

SERVES 2 TO 4

3¼ cups Clamato (clam-tomato juice)

¼ cup freshly squeezed lime juice (from 2 to 3 limes)

¾ teaspoon Tabasco sauce

Tajín seasoning, for rimming

1 lime wedge, for rimming

Ice

2 (12-ounce) bottles Mexican lager

Celery sticks, for garnish

If you like Bloody Marys, you're going to love this spicy Mexican beer cocktail. The key ingredient is Clamato, a brand of tomato juice seasoned with clam broth. It sounds strange, but trust me, it's savory and delicious. You top off the *micheladas* with a light beer such as a Mexican lager, which goes so well with the lime juice. It's the kind of bright and refreshing drink that will transport you to the beaches of Baja and make you go "*ahh*."

Combine the Clamato, lime juice, and Tabasco in a pitcher. Stir well and chill until ready to serve.

Place a layer of Tajín on a small plate. Moisten the rim of a tall glass with a lime wedge and dip it in the Tajín. Wiggle the glass to cover the wet part of the rim completely. Repeat to rim the remaining glass(es). Fill the glasses with ice and pour in the Clamato mixture. Add as much beer as you'd like and garnish each glass with a celery stick.

CHOCOLATE MINT COFFEE COCKTAILS

SERVES 4

3 cups whole milk

1 cup Kahlúa coffee liqueur

8 fresh chocolate mint leaves, plus more for garnish

¼ cup simple syrup (see page 24)

1 tablespoon unsweetened cocoa powder

Ice

Did you know there's actually a variety of mint that tastes like chocolate? I've been growing this herb in my garden for years, and I'm still so delighted and surprised every time I nibble on a leaf. It literally tastes like the chocolate-mint square they put on your pillow at a hotel. And that's what this after-dinner drink evokes—that treat you look forward to with turndown service, but right in your own home. Look for chocolate mint at your local nursery or farmers' market. In a pinch, you can use regular mint. The drink will still be amazing.

———————————

Combine the milk, Kahlúa, mint leaves, simple syrup, and cocoa powder in a blender. Blend until smooth. Fill four rocks glasses with ice. Strain the cocktail into the glasses and garnish with chocolate mint leaves. Alternatively, strain the cocktail into four coupe glasses.

STRAWBERRY, BASIL, and CARDAMOM MARGARITAS

SERVES 5 OR 6

3 cups water

2 cups chopped fresh strawberries, plus 5 or 6 whole berries for garnish

½ cup freshly squeezed lime juice (from about 5 limes)

¼ cup agave nectar

8 fresh basil leaves, plus 5 or 6 for garnish

5 fresh mint leaves

1 teaspoon ground cardamom

2 cups tequila blanco

Ice

Cardamom and I were not always the best of friends. I found it overpowering, like that one friend who constantly hogs the conversation. But I discovered that the key to getting along with this potent spice is to keep it in check (just like that friend). In this gorgeous margarita, I balance the peppery, citrusy cardamom with sweet strawberries and fresh basil. The combo is reminiscent of an intricate plated dessert. Bonus: Cardamom is great for digestion, making this a perfect drink either before or after a meal!

Combine the water, chopped strawberries, lime juice, agave, basil leaves, mint leaves, and cardamom in a blender. Blend until smooth. Strain the mixture into a large pitcher, then stir in the tequila. Fill five or six margarita or rocks glasses with ice and divide the margarita mixture among them. Garnish each glass with a basil leaf and a strawberry and serve.

PINEAPPLE-TURMERIC MARGARITAS

SERVES 4

1 tablespoon granulated sugar, for rimming

1 tablespoon chili powder, for rimming

3½ teaspoons ground turmeric

1 lime wedge

½ cup tequila blanco

2 cups pineapple juice

½ cup freshly squeezed lime juice (from about 5 limes)

¼ cup agave nectar, or to taste

Ice

4 fresh pineapple wedges and 8 pineapple leaves, for garnish

I've often proclaimed myself a tequila purist, and this is still true; sipping it neat in a small snifter accompanied by an orange wedge is how I typically enjoy the spirit. Lately, though, I've really been into margaritas and exploring different ingredients that highlight, not hide, the nuances of Mexico's most emblematic drink. Tequila can be earthy, as is turmeric. And we know that tequila loves tart flavors like citrus, so I added pineapple juice to come up with a balanced cocktail that lets each element shine.

Combine the sugar, chili powder, and 2 teaspoons of the turmeric on a small plate. Moisten the rim of a margarita or rocks glass with the lime wedge, then dip the rim in the chili-turmeric sugar. Wiggle the glass to cover the wet part of the rim completely. Repeat to rim three additional glasses.

Combine the tequila, pineapple juice, lime juice, agave nectar, and remaining 1½ teaspoons turmeric in a cocktail shaker. Fill with ice and shake until the outside of the shaker becomes frosty. Fill the rimmed glasses with ice and strain the margarita into them. Garnish each drink with a pineapple wedge and two pineapple leaves and enjoy!

WHITE PEACH SANGRIA

SERVES 6 TO 8

1 (750 ml) bottle semisweet white wine, such as Riesling, chilled

¾ cup simple syrup (see page 24)

¼ cup white rum

¼ cup freshly squeezed orange juice

1 cup fresh raspberries

2 fresh white peaches, pitted and sliced into wedges, plus 6 to 8 slices for garnish

6 to 8 fresh mint sprigs, for garnish

When you break out the sangria, that's when the party really starts. In the summer, I like to make a white version with sweet, aromatic white peaches at their peak. They bring out the best flavors in a slightly floral wine like Riesling. The raspberries give it a tart little kick, and look pretty in the glass to boot. This sangria is easy to make for a large group. You can even double the recipe, if you like!

Combine the wine, simple syrup, rum, and orange juice in a large pitcher. Stir in the raspberries and peach wedges. Cover and chill for at least 1 hour and up to 24 hours.

Fill six to eight wineglasses with ice and divide the sangria among them. Garnish each drink with a peach slice and a mint sprig and enjoy!

ROSEMARY-GRAPEFRUIT MIMOSAS

SERVES 8 TO 10

½ cup granulated sugar

½ cup water

3 sprigs fresh rosemary, plus more for garnish

3 cups unsweetened grapefruit juice, chilled

1 (750 ml) bottle champagne, chilled

Brunch is in these days—although, was it really ever out? People just love an excuse to push breakfast back a few hours and cure their hangover with the hair of the dog. And when mimosas are involved, who can blame them? I love the combo of tart, refreshing grapefruit with earthy, almost savory rosemary in this version. If you're not a fan of grapefruit, try blood orange juice for gorgeous color, or simply stick to the classic orange. Whatever citrus you choose, fresh juice is an absolute must!

Combine the sugar and water in a small saucepan. Bring to a simmer over medium heat and cook until the sugar has dissolved, about 4 minutes. Remove from the heat, add the rosemary sprigs, and let infuse for about 15 minutes. Remove the rosemary and let the syrup cool to room temperature.

For each mimosa, pour 1½ teaspoons of the rosemary syrup into a champagne flute. Fill the glasses halfway with grapefruit juice and top off with champagne. Garnish with a rosemary sprig and enjoy!

MEXICAN OLD-FASHIONED

SERVES 1

1 sugar cube

2 or 3 dashes of Angostura bitters

¼ cup tequila reposado

2 large ice cubes

1 (2-inch) strip orange zest (peeled with a vegetable peeler), for garnish

1 maraschino or brandied cherry, for garnish

My brother Antonio's favorite cocktail is an Old-Fashioned. He kept insisting I try his go-to drink, so I told him the only way I would is if it had tequila instead of the usual bourbon. And that, ladies and gentlemen, is how this Mexican Old-Fashioned was born. Orange, which is a traditional pairing with tequila in Mexico, works beautifully here. It brings out the smoky, rich flavor of the tequila reposado.

Put the sugar cube in a rocks glass. Dash the bitters directly onto the sugar cube and muddle until the cube disintegrates. Add the tequila and the ice cubes and stir well to combine. Rub the orange zest around the rim of the glass, then drop it in. Garnish with the cherry and enjoy!

HIBISCUS ICE POPS with PROSECCO

SERVES 8

1 cup dried hibiscus flowers
(flor de Jamaica)

3 cups water

¾ cup granulated sugar

1 (750 ml) bottle prosecco,
chilled

SPECIAL EQUIPMENT:

8 (¼-cup) ice pop molds

Jamaica or hibiscus flower water is a pretty common drink in Mexican households. It's like that lemonade you keep in the fridge and serve to your kids with lunch. The drink is a brilliant scarlet color and is always served over plenty of ice to bring out the flavor. It's also simple to freeze into *paletas* (ice pops). Add an ice pop to a glass of prosecco and it instantly becomes a fun, frosty cocktail that'll appeal to everyone's inner child.

In a medium heavy pot, combine the hibiscus flowers and water and bring the water to a boil over high heat, about 10 minutes. Remove from the heat. Add the sugar and stir until it has dissolved completely. Let cool. Strain the hibiscus flower water and reserve 16 of the steeped hibiscus flowers.

Place 2 hibiscus flowers in each ice pop mold and divide the hibiscus flower water evenly among the molds. Insert ice pop sticks, cover the molds, and freeze overnight or for up to 1 week.

Unmold the ice pops and place one in each of eight coupes or wineglasses. Fill each glass with prosecco and serve immediately.

FANCY PROSECCO GELATIN SHOTS with WHIPPED CREAM & STRAWBERRIES

MAKES 8 SHOTS

1½ cups prosecco

¼ cup granulated sugar

3 (¼-ounce) envelopes unflavored powdered gelatin

¼ cup vodka

Nonstick cooking spray

Whipped cream, for garnish

8 fresh strawberry slices, for garnish

8 mint sprigs, for garnish (optional)

Okay, I know what you may be thinking... "Jell-O shots? What, are we in college?" But hear me out: This boozy dessert is so sophisticated, it's like your dorm-room Jell-O shots went to charm school, then married a royal. The bubbly prosecco practically melts in your mouth. The best part? They're so easy to make, but they look like a million bucks. Your guests will love this bit of elevated nostalgia!

In a medium saucepan, stir together 1¼ cups of the prosecco and the sugar. Sprinkle in the gelatin and let stand for 2 minutes, until the gelatin has completely softened. Cook over low heat, stirring continuously, until the gelatin has completely dissolved, about 3 minutes. Remove from the heat and stir in the vodka and remaining ¼ cup prosecco. Let cool slightly.

Spray a glass loaf pan with cooking spray, pour in the prosecco mixture, cover, and refrigerate until firm, about 3 hours.

Turn the prosecco gelatin out onto a large cutting board. Cut it into eight 1-inch cubes and transfer to a serving platter. Top each cube with whipped cream, a strawberry slice and mint sprig, and serve.

SERRANO PORCH CRAWLERS

SERVES 4

½ cup granulated sugar

½ cup water

1 small serrano chile, seeded, plus seeded and thinly sliced chiles for garnish (optional)

2 (12-ounce) bottles Mexican lager, such as Corona

1 cup vodka

1 cup freshly squeezed lemon juice (from 5 or 6 lemons)

Ice

4 lemon wedges, for garnish

This is that refreshing drink that goes down real easy on a hot summer's day. If you've never tried chile in a cocktail, you're in for a treat. The first sip registers as sweet-tart, then the vodka kicks in, and THEN, right at the end, you feel a slow, subtle burn. The serrano chile flavor is mellow, but you know it's there—almost like it's telling you, "The party's not over yet!" I love drinks that have multiple layers of flavors, and this is certainly one of them!

In a small saucepan, combine the sugar and water and bring to a simmer over medium heat. Simmer until the sugar has dissolved, about 4 minutes. Remove from the heat, add the chile, and let infuse for about 15 minutes. Remove the chile and let the syrup cool completely.

Combine the serrano chile syrup, beer, vodka, and lemon juice in a large pitcher. Fill with ice and stir well to combine. Fill four collins glasses with ice and strain the drink into them. Garnish each with a lemon wedge, a few chile slices, and serve.

COFFEE ICE CREAM CARAJILLO with BURNT CINNAMON STICK

SERVES 8

1 quart coffee ice cream

2 cups Licor 43 (citrus and vanilla Spanish liqueur)

8 strips orange zest (peeled from 1 orange with a vegetable peeler)

8 cinnamon sticks

In my house, we love to unwind after dinner with a good drink to cleanse the palate. A *carajillo* does exactly that. It's traditionally served with a shot of espresso, but I up the ante with coffee ice cream. This could be considered dessert—that's how good it is. But here's the fun part: Grab a cinnamon stick and light the end, like you would with incense. Add it to the glass and let the intoxicating aromas make you fall in love with this drink.

Chill eight parfait cups or stemless wineglasses. Place a scoop of ice cream in each glass. Add ¼ cup of the Licor 43 and 1 strip of orange zest to each glass. Carefully light a cinnamon stick with a long-handled match or lighter. Extinguish the flame, add the cinnamon stick to a glass, then serve immediately. Repeat with the remaining cinnamon sticks.

BLOOD ORANGE PALOMA PITCHER

SERVES 6 TO 8

2 cups freshly squeezed
blood orange juice (from 6 or
7 blood oranges)

1½ cups sparkling water, chilled

1 cup tequila blanco

½ cup freshly squeezed lime
juice (from about 5 limes)

Simple syrup (see page 24)

Ice

Blood orange slices, for garnish

This is my big-batch take on a Paloma, the traditional Mexican cocktail of tequila and grapefruit. I have to confess, though, that it came about by accident. I was testing a classic Paloma recipe when I ran out of grapefruit. I decided to sub in blood oranges from my garden, and I dare say, this version might be even better than the original. Blood oranges have a deep, tangy-sweet flavor that's phenomenal with tequila. Not to mention, they give the drink a gorgeous color that makes everyone want to try it.

Combine the blood orange juice, sparkling water, tequila, and lime juice in a pitcher. Sweeten to taste with simple syrup and stir well. Fill six to eight glasses with ice and pour in the cocktail. Garnish each drink with a blood orange slice and serve.

KALIMOTXO
(RED WINE AND MEXICAN COKE SANGRIA)

SERVES 6 TO 8

½ cup granulated sugar

½ cup water

3 cinnamon sticks, plus more for garnish (optional)

1 (750 ml) bottle red wine

2 (355 ml) bottles Mexican Coca-Cola

¼ cup freshly squeezed lemon juice (from 1½ lemons)

Ice

6 to 8 lemon slices, for garnish

Fresh lavender flowers and edible flowers, for garnish (optional)

We are very influenced by Spain here in Mexico. Not only do we still have ancient European architecture in our country, we've also adopted our favorite Spanish dishes into our cuisine—like flan and sangria. *Kalimotxo* is a traditional Spanish red wine drink. Think of it as a sangria with Mexican Coke (the most delicious kind of Coke). Like sangria, *kalimotxo* is easy to make in advance. Citrusy and refreshing, this drink is a hit at summer barbecues.

In a small saucepan, combine the sugar, water, and cinnamon sticks and bring to a simmer over medium heat. Simmer until the sugar has dissolved, about 4 minutes. Remove from the heat and let infuse for about 15 minutes. Remove the cinnamon sticks and let the cinnamon syrup cool completely.

Combine the cinnamon syrup, wine, Coca-Cola, and lemon juice in a large pitcher. Stir well to combine. Fill six to eight glasses with ice and divide the kalimotxo among them. Garnish each drink with a lemon slice, cinnamon stick, lavender flower and edible flower, and serve.

MANDARIN-MINT MOJITOS

SERVES 6 TO 8

1 cup fresh mint leaves, plus 6 to 8 more for garnish

1 cup turbinado sugar, or to taste

10 ounces rum, or to taste

2 cups freshly squeezed mandarin orange juice (from 11 or 12 mandarins)

2 cups sparkling water, chilled

¼ cup freshly squeezed lime juice (from 2 or 3 limes)

Ice

Mandarin slices, for garnish (optional)

I am obsessed with mandarins. The perfect combination of tart and sweet, this citrus gives that extra something-something to cocktails. So I decided to add mandarin juice to this mojito variation that I make in one big batch. Not to pat myself on the back, but prepping this recipe in a pitcher is kind of brilliant, because it saves you the pain of muddling in individual glasses. That means you're not playing bartender all night *and* your guests get their drinks quicker—a win-win!

Combine the 1 cup mint leaves and sugar in a large pitcher; muddle until the mint leaves are crushed and the sugar starts to dissolve. Add the rum, mandarin juice, sparkling water, and lime juice. Add ice to the pitcher and stir well. Taste and add more rum or sugar if needed. Fill six to eight glasses with ice and strain the mojito into them. Garnish with mandarin slices and mint leaves and serve.

PEAR and VANILLA CHAMPAGNE COCKTAILS

SERVES 6

2 pears, peeled, cored, and cut into cubes

Juice of 1 lemon

1 vanilla bean, split lengthwise and seeds scraped out

Simple syrup (see page 24)

1 (750 ml) bottle champagne, chilled

6 pear slices, for garnish (optional)

6 (1-inch) strips of vanilla bean, for garnish (optional)

We are big fans of the bubbly over here at Casa Marcela. When I want to take champagne to the next level, I spike it with a fresh pear puree that I whip up in the blender. The sweetness of pears along with a dry champagne is a match made in heaven, but it's the vanilla bean in the puree that makes this drink so different and original. I like to serve this cocktail at brunch with the ladies. It makes us feel oh so fancy.

Combine the pears, lemon juice, and vanilla bean seeds in a blender. Blend until smooth and sweeten to taste with simple syrup. Divide the pear puree evenly among six coupes or champagne flutes. Top the glasses with champagne, garnish with pear slices and vanilla beans, and serve.

PROSECCO MARGARITAS

SERVES 4 TO 6

1½ cups freshly squeezed lime juice (from about 15 limes)

1 cup tequila blanco, or to taste

½ cup Cointreau

½ cup simple syrup (see page 24), or to taste

Coarse salt, for rimming

Lime slices, for rimming and for garnish

Ice

1 (750 ml) bottle prosecco, chilled

Yes, prosecco in your margarita. It adds that little something extra that a margarita sometimes needs. Don't get me wrong. I still love the OG classic, but when I want to switch it up, the bubbles make it feel special.

––––––––––––––––––––––––––

Combine the lime juice, tequila, Cointreau, and simple syrup in a pitcher. Stir well until combined.

Place a layer of salt on a small plate. Moisten the rim of a glass with a lime wedge and dip it in the salt. Wiggle the glass to cover the wet part of the rim completely. Repeat to rim the remaining glasses.

Fill the glasses with ice, then fill them halfway with the tequila-lime mixture. Top the glasses with the prosecco, garnish with lime slices, and serve.

KIR ROYALE PUNCH

SERVES 8 TO 10

2 (750 ml) bottles champagne, chilled

1 cup Chambord

1 cup freshly squeezed lemon juice (from 5 or 6 lemons)

1 cup fresh blackberries, for garnish

1 lemon, thinly sliced, for garnish

Ice

This is one fancy-sounding punch, but don't be fooled by its sophisticated name. It's one of the easiest drinks you'll ever make. A Kir royale is a bit of crème de cassis (black currant liqueur) in a glass topped with champagne. Here, I make a punch version using Chambord (a delicious black raspberry liqueur). Add bubbly and some fruit, and voila! The sweetness from the Chambord combined with the tanginess of lemons makes this a crowd favorite at Casa Marcela gatherings.

Combine the champagne, Chambord, and lemon juice in a large pitcher or bowl. Add the blackberries and lemon slices. Serve the punch in ice-filled glasses.

SOUR GHERKIN TAJÍN MARGARITAS

SERVES 6

½ cup Tajín seasoning, for rimming

2 tablespoons kosher salt, for rimming

Lime wedges, for rimming

3 cups water

2 cups Mexican sour gherkins (cucamelons)

1 cup freshly squeezed lime juice (from 10 limes)

5 fresh mint leaves

1½ cups tequila blanco

Simple syrup (see page 24)

Ice

Full disclosure: The sour gherkin plant in my garden went insane, and I had no idea what to do with the overabundance, so I blended them into margaritas. Also called "cucamelons," sour gherkins pretty much taste like cucumbers (just a little tangier), and in Mexico, cucumber is a common flavor variation for margaritas. You can find sour gherkins at farmers' markets, or plant them in your garden, where they'll grow like crazy! I love to give these margaritas a hit of tangy spice by rimming the glasses with Tajín, a chile-lime powder that you can find at Mexican markets. If it's not available, simply rim the glasses with a blend of cayenne pepper, salt, and lime zest.

Combine the Tajín and salt on a small plate. Moisten the rim of a margarita glass with a lime wedge. Dip the rim of the glass in the Tajín-salt mixture. Wiggle the glass to cover the wet part of the rim completely. Repeat to rim the remaining five glasses. Fill the glasses with ice and store them in the freezer until ready to serve.

Combine the water, sour gherkins, lime juice, and mint in a blender. Blend until smooth. Strain the sour gherkin limeade through a fine-mesh strainer set over a bowl, pressing down on the solids with a wooden spoon to extract all the liquid. Discard the solids.

For each margarita, combine ¼ cup of the tequila, ½ cup of the sour gherkin limeade, and simple syrup to taste in a cocktail shaker. Fill with ice and shake. Strain into a rimmed glass and enjoy!

WATERMELON FROSÉ

SERVES 6 TO 8

½ cup granulated sugar

½ cup water

Grated zest of 1 lemon, plus more for garnish (optional)

4 cups cubed fresh watermelon, frozen

1 (750 ml) bottle white zinfandel, chilled

Just close your eyes and imagine you're on a beach somewhere in the Mexican Caribbean. That's exactly where this drink transports me every time I take a sip. Basically a grown-up slushie, watermelon "frosé" refreshes you like an ocean wave on a hot summer day—no matter where you are.

In a small saucepan, combine the sugar and water and bring to a boil. Reduce the heat to maintain a simmer and cook until the sugar has completely dissolved, about 2 minutes. Remove from the heat. Add the lemon zest and let cool.

Working in batches, combine the cooled syrup, frozen watermelon, and wine in a blender and process until smooth. Pour into stemmed glasses, garnish with lemon zest, and serve immediately.

LAVENDER FRENCH 75

SERVES 1

1 ounce gin

½ ounce freshly squeezed lemon juice

½ ounce Lavender Syrup (recipe follows)

Ice

1 to 2 ounces dry sparkling wine, chilled

1 long, thin twist of lemon zest, for garnish

1 fresh lavender flower, for garnish (optional)

This cocktail is not just fancy, it's absolutely delicious. It's also not my recipe! When I was on the hunt for the perfect glassware for the photos in this book, someone directed me to Collins & Coupe in San Diego. This incredible store has both new and vintage barware and had me swooning over their one-of-a-kind pieces. Gary McIntire, who runs the shop, is the quintessential mixologist. He knows everything about spirits, mixers, glasses, equipment . . . so I was not surprised when I tested and fell in love with his take on the classic French 75! The lavender is subtle and lends an air of sophistication to this ultra-refreshing drink.

Combine the gin, lemon juice, and syrup in a shaker. Fill with ice, shake well, then strain into a flute or coupe glass. Top the glass with the sparkling wine, garnish with the lemon zest and lavender flower, and serve.

Lavender Syrup

2 cups water

2 cups granulated sugar

1 tablespoon dried culinary lavender

In a medium saucepan, combine all the ingredients. Bring to a boil over medium-high heat. Reduce the heat to low and simmer until the sugar has dissolved completely, about 2 minutes. Remove from the heat and let cool. Strain through a fine-mesh strainer or cheesecloth into a jar. Store in the refrigerator for up to 1 week. Any leftover syrup can be used to sweeten other drinks, such as lemonade or iced tea.

PITAYA MARGARITAS

SERVES 6 TO 8

4 cups water

1½ cups granulated sugar, or to taste

1 cup coarsely chopped pitaya (dragon fruit)

½ cup freshly squeezed lime juice (from about 5 limes)

Ice

2 cups tequila blanco

2 tablespoons kosher salt, for rimming

1 tablespoon crushed dried rose petals (preferably organic), for rimming

Lime wedges, for rimming

If you're not familiar with dragon fruit (also called pitaya), definitely give it a try in this cocktail. It has a flavor that's reminiscent of kiwi, but what's truly remarkable about it is its brilliant color—especially the kind that's fuchsia inside (instead of white). As with a lot of fruit-based drinks, you should taste the fruit for ripeness and then adjust the amount of sugar accordingly. (I'm pretty much used to making many of these cocktails without any added sugar at all.) And to take this margarita to the next level, I rim the glass with salt mixed with crushed dried rose petals. This is for sure a drink you want to Instagram before taking a sip.

Combine the water, sugar, pitaya, and lime juice in a blender. Blend until smooth. Transfer to a large pitcher and fill with ice. Add the tequila and stir well with a wooden spoon.

Combine the salt and crushed rose petals on a small plate. Moisten the rim of a glass with a lime wedge, then dip the rim in the rose salt. Wiggle the glass to coat the wet part of the rim completely. Repeat to rim the remaining glasses.

Fill the glasses with ice, strain the pitaya margarita into them, and serve.

dos: NIBBLES

CHILE-MANGO GUACAMOLE

SERVES 8

5 ripe but firm avocados, halved, pitted, and peeled

2 mangoes, pitted, peeled, and cubed (about 2 cups)

½ cup freshly squeezed lime juice (from 5 limes)

1 to 2 teaspoons red pepper flakes

1 teaspoon kosher salt

Chile oil, for garnish (optional)

Tortilla chips, for serving

I'm a guac purist but this is the rare deviation I happen to love. The mango is bright, citrusy, and fresh—the perfect foil for creamy, rich avocado. Then when the chile heat kicks in, that's when the flavor fiesta starts. No sane human can resist this combo with the salty crunch of tortilla chips. And right when you think you've figured out why you love this guacamole SO much, BOOM! You've just finished a whole bowl by yourself and you have nothing for your guests... Back to the kitchen for you!

Place the avocados in a medium bowl and roughly mash with a fork. Add the mangoes, lime juice, red pepper flakes, and salt. Stir gently until just combined. Drizzle the guacamole with chile oil, if desired, and serve with tortilla chips.

CHICKPEA CEVICHE TOSTADAS

MAKES 6 TOSTADAS

2 (15.5-ounce) cans chickpeas, drained and rinsed

2 medium tomatoes, cored and diced

1 medium zucchini, diced

1 scallion, chopped

1 fresh serrano chile, seeded, deveined, and minced

½ cup chopped fresh cilantro

½ cup freshly squeezed lime juice (from about 5 limes)

Kosher salt and freshly ground black pepper

6 tostadas, store-bought or homemade (see Note)

1 cup shredded lettuce

2 radishes, thinly sliced

Chipotle Tahini Sauce or Serrano Cilantro Tahini Sauce (recipes follow), for drizzling

I'm sorry to tell you, but these tostadas are good for you. And they're ::*whispers*:: vegan. But don't flip the page. They're amazing. (I actually make this dish weekly because it's such an awesome snack to have in the fridge.) I call this a "ceviche," even though it doesn't have lime-cured seafood, because it's a great way to let your guests know what flavors are coming. If you're familiar with ceviche, you know it's a citrusy mix of fresh and bright flavors. The chickpeas here give you the heft that you'd typically get from fish, but the dish is 100 percent plant-based. These days, there's a good chance you'll have a vegan or two at your get-together and they'll love you for this one!

Combine the chickpeas, tomatoes, zucchini, scallion, serrano, cilantro, and lime juice in a medium bowl. Toss and season to taste with salt and pepper. Refrigerate until you're ready to serve the tostadas.

Divide the chickpea ceviche among the tostadas and top with the shredded lettuce and a couple of radish slices. Drizzle with tahini sauce, and enjoy!

note

To make your own tostadas, bake 6 corn tortillas on a baking sheet in a 400°F oven until crispy and golden brown, about 10 minutes.

Chipotle Tahini Sauce

MAKES ABOUT 1 CUP

½ cup tahini

½ cup water

2 tablespoons pure maple syrup

1 tablespoon rice vinegar

1 whole canned chipotle chile in adobo sauce

1 tablespoon grated lime zest

Kosher salt and freshly ground black pepper

Combine the tahini, water, maple syrup, vinegar, chipotle, and lime zest in a food processor. Process until smooth. Season generously with salt and pepper. The tahini sauce can be refrigerated for up to 2 days.

Serrano Cilantro Tahini Sauce

MAKES ABOUT 1 CUP

½ cup tahini

½ cup water

1 tablespoon rice vinegar

1 fresh serrano chile, seeded

½ cup chopped fresh cilantro

¼ cup freshly squeezed lime juice (from 2 or 3 limes)

Kosher salt and freshly ground black pepper

Combine the tahini, water, vinegar, serrano, cilantro, and lime juice in a food processor. Process until smooth. Season generously with salt and pepper. The tahini sauce can be refrigerated for up to 2 days.

BUTTERNUT SQUASH GOAT CHEESE BITES

MAKES 20 PASTRIES

2½ cups cubed peeled butternut squash

½ cup olive oil

2 garlic cloves, minced

2 tablespoons agave nectar

½ teaspoon chipotle powder

Kosher salt and freshly ground black pepper

1 (17.3-ounce) package frozen puff pastry (2 sheets), thawed

1 large egg, beaten with 1 tablespoon water

4 ounces fresh goat cheese, crumbled

Chopped fresh chives, for garnish

Simple, classic flavor combos are always a hit because your guests know what to expect from them. Here I pair smooth, creamy roasted butternut squash with tangy goat cheese to top crisp, buttery puff pastry. A little bit of chipotle powder adds a smoky heat to the sweet caramelized squash. When it's just you, a friend, and a bottle of wine, these pastries are easy, delicious, and super satisfying. As for the puff pastry, you can go ahead and DIY it, but the frozen kind they have at the supermarket is so good, I don't see why you would!

Preheat the oven to 375°F. Line two rimmed baking sheets with parchment paper.

Combine the butternut squash, olive oil, garlic, agave, and chipotle powder in a medium bowl. Toss to coat the squash. Season to taste with salt and pepper. Transfer the squash to one of the prepared baking sheets and bake for about 45 minutes, until fork-tender and caramelized. Remove from the oven and let cool. Keep the oven on.

Place the puff pastry sheets on a work surface. Cut each sheet into 10 even rectangles, about 3 x 4.5 inches. Transfer to the prepared baking sheet. Prick the pastry rectangles all over with a fork. Brush each rectangle with the beaten egg and top them with the goat cheese and butternut squash, dividing them evenly among the rectangles. Bake for 20 to 25 minutes, until the pastry is puffed and golden brown. Remove from the oven and serve on your favorite platter, garnished with the chopped chives.

MUSHROOM-WALNUT PÂTÉ

MAKES ABOUT 2 CUPS

1 cup walnut pieces

1 tablespoon coconut oil

½ medium onion, diced

1 garlic clove, minced

1 pound cremini mushrooms, sliced

2 sprigs fresh thyme, chopped, plus an extra sprig, for garnish (optional)

1 sprig fresh rosemary, chopped

1 tablespoon tamari

2 teaspoons rice vinegar

Kosher salt and freshly ground black pepper

Your favorite crackers or baguette toasts, for serving

Warning: This spread is completely addictive. At the first bite, you're like, *Hmm . . . what is this? It looks and feels like pâté, but it's nutty, earthy, and intriguing.* Then you have another bite, and another, and you don't stop until you've eaten the whole thing. But seriously, this dish is exactly what you want to have at a fancy gathering. It can take the place of a traditional pâté or be served alongside, as the two can share crackers. It's a fantastic option for your vegan/vegetarian guests but will surely be devoured by all.

In a medium skillet, toast the walnuts over medium heat, shaking the pan often to prevent them from burning, until the nuts start to brown, 5 to 7 minutes. Transfer the nuts to a plate to cool.

In the same pan, melt the coconut oil over medium heat. Add the onion and garlic and cook, stirring, until the onion is translucent, 3 to 5 minutes. Add the mushrooms and herbs. Cook, stirring, until the mushrooms are tender, 5 to 7 minutes, adding 1 tablespoon water if the mushrooms begin to stick to the pan.

Transfer the toasted walnuts to a food processor and process for about 30 seconds. Add the sautéed mushrooms, tamari, and vinegar and pulse, stopping and scraping down the food processor bowl as necessary, until the mixture has the consistency of pâté. You don't want it completely smooth; the pâté should still have some texture to it. Season to taste with salt and pepper. Transfer the pâté to a small bowl and serve with your favorite crackers or baguette toasts.

SWEET POTATO CHIPOTLE HUMMUS

MAKES ABOUT 2 CUPS

1 large sweet potato, peeled and cut into 1-inch pieces

Kosher salt

1 (15.5-ounce) can chickpeas, drained and rinsed

3 tablespoons extra-virgin olive oil, plus more for drizzling

3 tablespoons tahini

3 garlic cloves

1 tablespoon grated lemon zest

¼ cup freshly squeezed lemon juice (from 1½ lemons)

1 teaspoon chopped fresh thyme

1½ teaspoons chipotle powder

Paprika, for garnish

Pita chips, for serving

Everyone—young and old, from vegans to meat lovers—is happy to have hummus at a party. I like to jazz up my version with sweet potatoes spiked with smoky chipotle powder. This dip is fantastic with pita chips or anything crunchy, like celery or tortilla chips. It goes like gangbusters at gatherings, but if you have any left over, the hummus is amazing on toast the next day, topped with a fried egg, avocado slices, a drizzle of olive oil, and a sprinkle of sea salt. The hummus is best made a day ahead and chilled. Just bring it to room temperature before serving.

Place the sweet potato in a large pot and cover with 2 inches of salted water. Bring to a boil over high heat. Reduce the heat to medium-low and simmer until the sweet potato is very tender, about 15 minutes. Drain and let cool to room temperature. Transfer the sweet potato to a food processor. Add the chickpeas, olive oil, tahini, garlic, lemon zest, lemon juice, thyme, and chipotle powder and process until smooth. Season to taste with salt. Transfer the hummus to a serving bowl, drizzle with additional olive oil, and sprinkle with paprika. Serve with pita chips.

ROASTED CORN, ZUCCHINI, and JALAPEÑO SALAD

SERVES 6 TO 8

¾ cup extra-virgin olive oil

Lime wedge, for garnish, plus ¼ cup freshly squeezed lime juice (from 2 or 3 limes)

Kosher salt and freshly ground black pepper

4 ears corn, roasted, kernels cut off

4 large zucchini, chopped into small pieces

1 jalapeño, stemmed, seeded, and finely chopped

½ cup finely chopped fresh cilantro

1 chive blossom (optional), for garnish

1 cup chicharrón (pork cracklings), for serving

Here's the thing about entertaining: You always have to have a salad. Always. But how do you get people to eat vegetables when there are chips, dips, and cheese to tempt them? You make a salad with corn that's been roasted to bring out its natural sweetness. Toss in some lime and chiles, and the combo is reminiscent of Mexican street corn—which just about everyone loves!

Place the olive oil and lime juice in a small bowl. Whisk until combined and season to taste with salt and pepper.

Combine the corn kernels, zucchini, jalapeño, and cilantro in a large bowl. Toss with the lime dressing until combined. Season to taste with salt and pepper. Cover and refrigerate before serving for at least 2 hours and up to 1 day. Transfer to a serving bowl, top with the lime wedge and chive blossom, and serve with the chicharrón alongside for dipping.

CRISPY ROASTED CHIPOTLE CHICKPEAS

**MAKES ABOUT
3½ CUPS**

Nonstick cooking spray

2 (15.5-ounce) cans chickpeas, drained and rinsed

2 tablespoons extra-virgin olive oil

2 teaspoons chipotle powder

2 teaspoons grated lemon zest

2 teaspoons kosher salt

These fun little spiced chickpeas are like high-protein popcorn—highly snackable. Set them at the bar to have with beer or cocktails. (They also happen to be a terrific after-school snack . . . but who wants to be reminded about cooking for your picky kids while party planning? I apologize.) If you roast the chickpeas a day ahead, just store them in an airtight container and they're good to go when you need them!

Preheat the oven to 350°F and place the rack in the center of the oven. Spray a rimmed baking sheet with cooking spray.

Dry the chickpeas with paper towels. Toss the chickpeas, olive oil, chipotle powder, lemon zest, and salt in a medium bowl. Transfer to the prepared baking sheet, spreading the chickpeas out in one layer. This will help prevent them from sticking to one another and ensure they cook evenly.

Bake for 50 minutes to 1 hour. Halfway through baking, move the chickpeas around with a spatula. When the chickpeas are slightly crisp and golden brown, remove from the oven and let cool for about 1 hour before serving. They will become crunchier as they cool. Transfer to your favorite bowl and serve as an appetizer, or store them in an airtight container and take them on the go as a snack.

BAKED ARTICHOKE DIP

MAKES ABOUT 4 CUPS

1 (8-ounce) can marinated artichoke hearts, drained and coarsely chopped

1 cup mayonnaise

½ cup grated Parmesan cheese

4 ounces cream cheese, at room temperature

1 teaspoon dried dill

½ teaspoon garlic powder

Kosher salt and freshly ground black pepper

Baguette toasts, for serving

This is a traditional, straightforward artichoke dip, but it's so good, your guests will park themselves right beside it throughout the party. It's impossible to resist the creamy, cheesy dip—especially slathered on crunchy baguette toasts.

Preheat the oven to 375°F. Combine the artichokes, mayonnaise, Parmesan cheese, cream cheese, dill, and garlic powder in a medium bowl. Mix until all the ingredients are incorporated. Season to taste with salt and pepper. (At this point, the dip can be covered and refrigerated for up to 1 day.)

Transfer the dip to an oven-safe ramekin or bowl and bake for about 30 minutes, or until the top is golden brown. Place the ramekin on a platter and serve the dip warm with the baguette toasts alongside.

BUTTERNUT SQUASH LATKES

MAKES ABOUT 20 LATKES

5 cups grated butternut squash

⅔ cup all-purpose flour

2 large eggs, beaten

½ teaspoon kosher salt

½ teaspoon freshly ground black pepper

½ teaspoon garlic powder

1 tablespoon finely chopped fresh basil

Olive oil, for frying

Crème fraîche, for serving

Caviar, for serving (optional)

Lemon wedges (optional), for garnish

Finely chopped fresh chives and chive blossoms (optional), for garnish

I know this dish is a home run because when I had my son David's godparents over, I set these latkes out and they were gone in the time it took me to fetch a glass of wine. It didn't hurt that I had some leftover caviar and crème fraîche from another holiday party to dollop on the latkes. (You could just as easily use smoked salmon and sour cream or Mexican crema.) I now make these latkes ahead of time and keep them in the freezer for any last-minute guests.

Combine the butternut squash, flour, eggs, salt, pepper, garlic powder, and basil in a large bowl. Stir until combined.

Pour enough olive oil into a large sauté pan to coat the bottom and place over medium-high heat. Once the oil is hot, spoon the butternut squash mixture in mounds (2 tablespoons each) into the oil, making sure to space them about 2 inches apart (this will give you enough room to flip the latkes and prevent them from sticking to one another). Firmly press down on each latke with a spatula to flatten. Fry the latkes until golden brown and crisp, 2 to 3 minutes on each side. Transfer the latkes to a plate lined with paper towels to drain the excess oil. Fry the remaining latkes in batches.

Transfer to a platter and top the latkes with the crème fraîche, caviar, lemon wedges, and chives and blossoms. Serve immediately.

GRILLED BRIE STUFFED with PILONCILLO- CARAMELIZED APPLES

SERVES 6

1 tablespoon unsalted butter

1 cup thinly sliced apples

2 fresh thyme sprigs

2 fresh rosemary sprigs

½ cup piloncillo (unrefined whole cane sugar; available at Latin markets)

1 (16-ounce) wheel of Brie, chilled

2 tablespoons extra-virgin olive oil

Crackers or sliced baguette, for serving

If you like baked Brie, you are going to swoon over this Brie sandwiched with sautéed apples. Just imagine taking your whole cheese board and throwing it on the grill. (I have been known to skip dinner and just have this gooey cheese goodness as my meal.) To get those beautiful char marks on the Brie, make sure the grill is screaming hot. Otherwise, the cheese will melt into the grates and create a literal hot mess. If you want to add a little smoke, stem, seed, and thinly slice some guajillo chiles and toss them in with the apples before they caramelize. I love to prep everything the day before, then just assemble and slap the Brie on the grill at the party. And do yourself a favor: Plan a menu that takes advantage of the grill being fired up!

———

Heat an outdoor grill to 500°F or a stovetop grill pan over medium-low heat.

Meanwhile, melt the butter in a medium saucepan over medium-low heat. Add the apples, thyme, and rosemary and sauté until the apples are slightly tender, about 5 minutes. Add the piloncillo and cook until the piloncillo starts to caramelize, about 5 minutes. Remove from the heat. Pick out the thyme and rosemary and discard. Let the apples cool.

recipe continues

Meanwhile, slice the wheel of Brie in half horizontally so you have 2 circles of cheese. Put the apples on the cut side of one circle, then top with the other circle, cut-side down.

Brush the grill grates or pan with the olive oil. Transfer the wheel of Brie to the grill and cook for about 3 minutes on each side, or until grill marks appear on the cheese rind. Transfer to a platter and serve immediately with a sliced baguette or your favorite crackers.

GOAT CHEESE-STUFFED FRIED OLIVES

MAKES 30 OLIVES

2 ounces fresh goat cheese, at room temperature

1 teaspoon dried Mexican oregano

Kosher salt and freshly ground black pepper

30 pitted large green olives, rinsed and dried thoroughly

Vegetable oil, for frying

½ cup all-purpose flour

2 large eggs, lightly beaten

¾ cup panko bread crumbs

2 teaspoons ancho chile powder

My love-hate relationship with goat cheese is as intense as something in a Mexican telenovela. Now we're definitely on again. The goat cheese gets fried and melty and, well . . . I'm only human, after all. You can use any olives that are large enough to stuff. Also, make sure to dry the olives completely so the coating doesn't fall off or get bald spots.

Combine the goat cheese and oregano in a small bowl and mix until smooth. Season to taste with salt and pepper. Transfer to a pastry bag fitted with a plain round tip. Pipe about ½ teaspoon of goat cheese into each olive. Set aside.

Pour enough vegetable oil into a heavy large saucepan to come halfway up the sides of the pan and heat the oil to 375°F. Meanwhile, spread the flour on a large plate and set aside. Place the eggs in a shallow bowl. Combine the panko and ancho chile powder on a large plate and season with salt and pepper.

Roll the olives in the flour, coating them all over and shaking off the excess. Then dip them in the egg, letting any excess drip back into the bowl. Finally coat the olives all over with the chile bread crumbs.

Transfer the olives to the pan and fry until golden brown, about 1 minute. Remove from the oil using a slotted spoon and transfer to a plate lined with paper towels to drain the excess oil. Transfer to a platter and serve warm or at room temperature.

EMPANADAS DE RAJAS

(POBLANO AND CREAM CHEESE EMPANADAS)

MAKES 10 TO 12 EMPANADAS

6 fresh poblano chiles

1 tablespoon unsalted butter

½ medium onion, thinly sliced

1 (8-ounce) package cream cheese

Kosher salt

1 (17.3 ounces) package frozen puff pastry, thawed

1 large egg, beaten with 1 tablespoon water

SPECIAL EQUIPMENT:

5-inch round cookie cutter

I always serve puff pastry empanadas at my gatherings because they are so easy to make. You can literally take any two ingredients that work well together, stuff them in dough, and boom! You've got super-tasty empanadas. Having a soft, cheesy component is key. Here I use cream cheese, which may not be the most traditional filling, but I like how it spreads and holds up nicely in the oven. It's great for entertaining because the resulting empanadas don't need to be eaten right away—they're best about 15 minutes after baking, when they're not as hot as the sun but still warm, and the cheese is soft. I pair the cream cheese with *rajas* (strips of roasted poblanos). The smell of these chiles being charred has to be one of my favorites ever. I'd never leave a party if I walked in and was greeted by that aroma.

Preheat the oven to 400°F. Line a baking sheet with parchment paper.

Char the poblano chiles directly over a gas flame on the stove or under the broiler, turning them frequently with tongs, until blistered and charred all over. Transfer the poblanos to a zip-top bag and seal to let them steam and cool for about 10 minutes.

Peel the poblanos, then cut off the tops to remove the seeds and ribs. Slice the poblanos into ¼ to ½-inch strips.

Melt the butter in a medium saucepan over medium heat. Add the onion and cook, stirring, until translucent, about 5 minutes. Add the poblano strips and cook until the flavors blend, about 6 more minutes. Stir in the cream cheese until it has completely melted. Season to taste with salt. Remove from the heat and set aside.

Unfold one of the puff pastry sheets on a lightly floured work surface and, using a floured rolling pin, roll it out to ¼ inch thick. Using the cutter, stamp out 5 or 6 circles. Repeat with the remaining puff pastry sheet. Spoon 1 tablespoon of the poblano filling onto the center of each round of pastry. Brush the edge of each pastry circle with the beaten egg and fold in half to form a half-moon. Using a fork, press to seal the edges.

Arrange the empanadas on the prepared baking sheet and brush them with the remaining beaten egg. Bake until golden brown, 10 to 12 minutes. Remove from the oven, transfer to a platter, and serve warm.

ULTIMATE SPRING CRUDITÉS PLATTER

SERVES 8 TO 10

Carrots, cut into sticks

Celery, cut into sticks

Radishes

Cucumbers, sliced into spears

Grape tomatoes

Snap peas

Beer-Battered Asparagus (recipe follows)

Spicy Chimichurri (recipe follows)

Jalapeño-Cilantro Aioli (recipe follows)

Chipotle Mayo Hummus (recipe follows)

I have a rather large garden, and sometimes I end up with way more vegetables than I know what to do with. So to showcase their just-picked flavor, I arrange them on a crudités platter. I realize not everyone has a garden but almost everyone has access to a farmers' market. Head over there and talk to the vendors. Pick the fresh stuff and go to town. As a general rule, younger (smaller) veggies are sweeter and more delicious when raw than larger, mature ones. I like to serve crudités with two kinds of dip—in this case, a smoky chipotle hummus and a bright jalapeño-cilantro aioli. I also top the veggies with a spicy chimichurri to give them a vinegary kick. It works great with either dip or with no dip at all!

Place the raw vegetables and asparagus on a large serving platter. Drizzle the raw vegetables with the Spicy Chimichurri. Serve with the Jalapeño-Cilantro Aioli and Chipotle Mayo Hummus and enjoy!

Beer-Battered Asparagus

Vegetable oil, for frying

1 cup all-purpose flour

1 teaspoon dried basil

1 teaspoon dried rosemary

1 teaspoon dried Mexican oregano

¼ teaspoon kosher salt

½ teaspoon freshly ground black pepper

1 cup lager beer, at room temperature

1 pound asparagus

Pour enough vegetable oil into a large heavy skillet to come about 3 inches up the side of the pan and heat the oil to 350°F.

Meanwhile, combine the flour, basil, rosemary, oregano, salt, and pepper in a medium bowl. Gradually add the beer and whisk until combined.

Dip the asparagus into the beer batter and transfer to the skillet in small batches. Fry until golden brown, 2 to 3 minutes per batch. Transfer to a plate lined with paper towels to drain the excess oil.

Jalapeño-Cilantro Aioli

¾ cup mayonnaise

½ cup firmly packed fresh cilantro, plus more for garnish

1 jalapeño, seeded and diced

1 garlic clove

2 teaspoons grated lime zest

2 tablespoons freshly squeezed lime juice

Kosher salt and freshly ground black pepper

Extra-virgin olive oil, for drizzling

Place the mayonnaise, cilantro, jalapeño, garlic, lime zest, and lime juice in a blender or food processor and process until smooth. Season to taste with salt and pepper. Transfer the aioli to a serving bowl, cover, and refrigerate for up to 1 day before serving. Drizzle with olive oil and garnish with cilantro just before serving.

Chipotle Mayo Hummus

2 (15.5-ounce) cans chickpeas, drained and rinsed

¾ cup mayonnaise

½ cup water

¼ cup tahini

1 red bell pepper, coarsely chopped

3 tablespoons freshly squeezed lemon juice

2 tablespoons extra-virgin olive oil

1 tablespoon adobe sauce (from a can of chipotle chiles in adobo)

2 garlic cloves

Kosher salt and freshly ground black pepper

Place the chickpeas, mayonnaise, water, tahini, bell pepper, lemon juice, olive oil, adobo sauce, and garlic in a food processor and process until smooth. Season to taste with salt and black pepper. Transfer the hummus to a serving bowl, cover, and refrigerate for up to 1 day before serving.

Spicy Chimichurri

4 garlic cloves, unpeeled

½ cup extra-virgin olive oil, plus more for drizzling

1 teaspoon kosher salt, plus more for seasoning

1 cup packed fresh parsley

½ cup packed fresh cilantro

1 shallot, chopped

2 small dried chiles (such as chiles de árbol), crushed

½ teaspoon freshly ground black pepper

⅓ cup red wine vinegar

Preheat the oven to 350°F. Place the garlic cloves on a piece of aluminum foil large enough to wrap the garlic. Add a drizzle of olive oil and a pinch of salt. Wrap tightly and roast in the oven until the garlic is golden and completely soft, 20 to 25 minutes. Remove from the oven, let cool, then peel and transfer the roasted garlic to a food processor.

Add the parsley, cilantro, shallot, crushed chiles, salt, and pepper to the food processor. Pulse for 5 to 10 seconds to combine. With the machine running, slowly add the vinegar, then the olive oil. The chimichurri can be refrigerated overnight. Bring to room temperature before serving.

TRIO of VEGGIE TACOS on ZUCCHINI TORTILLAS

SERVES 8

CREAMED POBLANO FILLING

2 tablespoons coconut oil

½ medium white onion, thinly sliced

2 cups fresh or thawed frozen corn kernels (from about 2 ears, if fresh)

6 fresh poblano chiles, charred (over a gas burner or under the broiler), peeled, seeded, and thinly sliced

2 cups Cashew Cream (recipe follows)

Kosher salt

KALE AND SWEET POTATO FILLING

2 tablespoons coconut oil

1 garlic clove, minced

1 cup cubed peeled sweet potato

2 teaspoons chipotle powder

Kosher salt and freshly ground black pepper

2 cups chopped kale leaves

PORTOBELLO MUSHROOM FILLING

2 tablespoons coconut oil

3 portobello mushrooms, sliced

2 tablespoons balsamic vinegar

Kosher salt and freshly ground black pepper

Jalapeño-Cilantro Cashew Cream (recipe follows), for serving

Zucchini Tortillas (recipe follows), for serving

These are the fanciest tacos you will ever lay your eyes on. Yes, they are vegetarian. I know. If you had mentioned vegetarian tacos to me a few years ago, I would have screamed, "BLASPHEMY!" But here I am, telling you these are absolutely addictive. I like to serve them with the three different fillings to showcase a variety of vegetables that are distinct yet work so well together. You'll get an array of flavors: spicy, smoky, vinegary, sweet, savory, and fresh! Of course, if you just want to focus on one or two of the toppings, that's completely fine. Also, if I were you, I would make extra zucchini tortillas and freeze them, because they'll work with pretty much any taco filling.

I actually like to snack on them on their own or stuffed with avocado slices and sprinkled with salt. And by all means, throw some chicken in there if it makes you happy, but I really think the veggie ones are perfect as is!

FOR THE CREAMED POBLANO FILLING, melt the coconut oil in a medium saucepan over medium-high heat. Add the onion and cook, stirring, until translucent, about 5 minutes. Add the corn and poblanos and cook, stirring, for another 5 minutes. Add 2 cups of the cashew cream and simmer until thick, about 3 minutes. Season to taste with salt. Remove from the heat and set aside.

FOR THE KALE AND SWEET POTATO FILLING, melt the coconut oil in a medium saucepan over medium heat. Add the garlic and cook, stirring, for about 2 minutes. Add the sweet potato and cook, stirring occasionally, until lightly browned, 5 to 7 minutes. Add the chipotle powder and cook, stirring occasionally, until the sweet potato starts to soften, 8 to 10 minutes. Season with salt and pepper. Add the kale and cover the pan. Reduce the heat to low and simmer until the kale wilts slightly, 3 to 5 minutes. Season the filling to taste with salt and pepper. Remove from the heat and set aside.

FOR THE PORTOBELLO MUSHROOM FILLING, melt the coconut oil in a medium saucepan over medium heat. Add the mushrooms and cook until they start to soften, about 5 minutes. Add the vinegar and season with salt and pepper. Cook for about 2 more minutes, until the vinegar has reduced. Season to taste with salt and pepper. Remove from the heat and set aside.

TO ASSEMBLE THE TACOS, grab a zucchini tortilla and top it with your favorite filling. Drizzle the portobello tacos with some Jalapeño-Cilantro Cashew Cream.

Zucchini Tortillas

MAKES ABOUT 8 TORTILLAS

Coconut oil, for greasing

4 cups coarsely grated zucchini (about 2 pounds or 6 medium zucchini)

1 cup shredded mozzarella cheese

1 large egg

½ teaspoon coarsely ground black pepper

¼ teaspoon sea salt

¼ teaspoon garlic powder

Preheat the oven to 450°F. Line two baking sheets with parchment paper and grease with coconut oil.

Wrap the grated zucchini in cheesecloth or a kitchen towel and squeeze out as much liquid as possible. (Removing the excess moisture will help the tortillas stay intact during baking.) Transfer the zucchini to a large bowl. Add the mozzarella, egg, pepper, salt, and garlic powder. Mix to combine.

Using an ice cream scoop, scoop the zucchini mixture onto the parchment paper. Press each mound into a thin circle, about 5 inches in diameter. Bake for 20 to 25 minutes, until the tortillas begin to brown around the edges. Remove from the oven and let cool. Carefully peel the zucchini tortillas from the parchment and transfer to a serving platter.

Cashew Cream

2 cups raw cashews

2 cups water, plus more as needed

Soak the cashews in the water for about 3 hours. Strain the cashews, reserving the soaking liquid. Transfer the cashews to a blender or food processor and process until smooth. With the machine running, gradually add the reserved soaking liquid until the cashew cream reaches your desired consistency. (If you run out of soaking liquid, add more water, if necessary.) The cashew cream can be refrigerated for up to 2 days. Whisk or blend to re-emulsify.

Jalapeño-Cilantro Cashew Cream

2 cups raw cashews

2 cups water, plus more as needed

1 jalapeño, seeded

1 cup fresh cilantro

1 tablespoon grated lime zest

Kosher salt and freshly ground black pepper

Soak the cashews in the water for about 3 hours. Strain the cashews, reserving the soaking liquid. Transfer the cashews to a blender or food processor and process until smooth. With the machine running, gradually add the reserved soaking liquid until the cashew cream reaches your desired consistency. (If you run out of soaking liquid, add more water if necessary.) Add the jalapeño, cilantro, and lime zest and blend until incorporated. Season to taste with salt and pepper. The cashew cream can be refrigerated for up to 2 days. Whisk or blend to re-emulsify.

CILANTRO and JALAPEÑO MOUSSE

SERVES 10 TO 12

2¼ cups loosely packed fresh cilantro leaves (from 1½ bunches)

2 (8-ounce) packages cream cheese, at room temperature

3 green onions, white and pale green parts only, thinly sliced

¼ cup freshly squeezed lime juice (from 2 or 3 limes)

1 whole pickled jalapeño, plus 3 tablespoons pickling liquid from the can

1 tablespoon soy sauce

1 tablespoon mayonnaise

1½ teaspoons kosher salt

2 tablespoons cold water

1 (¼-ounce) envelope unflavored powdered gelatin

¼ cup hot water

Crackers, for serving

I need to warn you: Guests won't be able to tear themselves away from this dish. It's citrusy, fresh, and spicy with a hint of jalapeño. Served in its container, this mousse is more like a spread. You can make the mousse in one large dish or divide it into small ramekins if you want to set it out on multiple tables. The mousse keeps well chilled for a couple of days. Just cover it tightly with plastic wrap so it doesn't absorb any other flavors in the fridge. In the unlikely event you have any leftover mousse, smear it on toast for the best cucumber sandwich you've ever had.

Place the cilantro, cream cheese, green onions, lime juice, pickled jalapeño, pickling liquid, soy sauce, mayonnaise, and salt in a blender and blend until smooth.

Put the cold water in a small bowl and sprinkle the gelatin over the water; stir until smooth and all the lumps have dissolved. Add the hot water to soften the gelatin and stir until smooth.

Add the gelatin to the mixture in the blender and blend until well combined. Pour the mixture into a serving dish or divide it evenly among smaller ramekins.

Cover with plastic wrap and refrigerate until firm, about 2 hours. Let the mousse stand at room temperature for 20 minutes, then discard the plastic wrap, unmold the mousse onto a platter (if you used a larger dish) or smaller plates (if you used ramekins), and serve with crackers.

PHILIP'S MULTIPURPOSE TOMATO SAUCE

MAKES 4 CUPS,
OR ENOUGH FOR 8
TO 10 FIRST-COURSE
SERVINGS
OF SPAGHETTI

¼ cup plus 2 tablespoons extra-virgin olive oil

5 garlic cloves, minced

2 small shallots, coarsely chopped

4 pounds vine-ripened tomatoes, chopped

1 (28-ounce) can diced San Marzano tomatoes

½ cup beef stock

Kosher salt

2 tablespoons light brown sugar, or to taste

5 fresh basil leaves

This sauce sure isn't Mexican, but it is what we have the most at home. And I don't even have to lift a finger for it. My fiancé, Philip, has been perfecting this recipe since he started cooking from our garden a few years ago. Nothing on earth tastes quite like a freshly plucked vine-ripened tomato at its peak: sweet as candy, with flesh so soft it melts like butter into the sauce. When Philip simmers a huge batch, he nurses it, talks to it . . . might add a pinch of sugar if the tomatoes are store-bought and need a little help. We use half the sauce for pizzas, pasta, and calzones, then freeze the rest in zip-top bags. It's become a huge lifesaver for last-minute entertaining. I cannot tell you how many times I've pulled a bag from the freezer when a dinner for four turned into a party of ten on a moment's notice. This sauce has brought so much to our family! Probably one of the bigger reasons I said yes when he got down on one knee! It stars in one of our favorite appetizers, which we learned from our friend in France, Oddur Thorisson: Boil a pound of spaghetti and divide it into small bowls (about ⅓ cup of pasta for each portion). Then top generously with the sauce (thawed from one freezer bag), Parmesan cheese, a fresh basil leaf, and drizzle on some really good olive oil. This simple dish is an unexpected but killer first course for your next get-together.

Heat ¼ cup of the oil in a heavy medium pot over medium heat. Add the garlic and shallots and cook, stirring, until fragrant, about 6 minutes. Add the fresh and canned tomatoes and the stock and stir to combine. Season to taste with salt. Add the remaining 2 tablespoons olive oil, the brown sugar, and the basil and bring the sauce to a boil. Reduce the heat to low and simmer for 2 hours, until the sauce has thickened and is a deep red color. Serve immediately or let cool then divide the sauce among zip-top bags and freeze for up to 3 months.

BLACK BEAN SOUP SHOTS with TOASTED PEPITAS

MAKES 12 SHOTS

2 (15-ounce) cans black beans, drained and rinsed

1¾ cups water

2 teaspoons garlic powder

Kosher salt and freshly ground black pepper

¼ cup crema (Mexican sour cream)

¼ cup pepitas (pumpkin seeds), toasted

SPECIAL EQUIPMENT:

12 shot glasses

Beans are the caviar of Mexican food, and I like to treat them with due respect in this creamy, satisfying soup: just a good sprinkling of salt to bring out the flavor, a touch of tangy Mexican crema (or sour cream or crème fraîche), and that's pretty much it, my friends. To make the presentation fun for parties, I serve the soup in shot glasses—no need to mess with spoons! For some crunch, I garnish the soup with toasted pepitas (pumpkin seeds), but fried tortilla strips would be delicious, too.

Combine the black beans and water in a small pot. Bring to a boil over medium-high heat, then reduce the heat to low and simmer for about 5 minutes. Transfer to a blender and add the garlic powder. Carefully blend until smooth. Season to taste with salt and pepper. Pour the soup into the shot glasses, garnish each with a dollop of Mexican crema and a sprinkling of pepitas, and serve right away.

MUSHROOM-THYME QUESADILLAS

MAKES 3 QUESADILLAS

4 tablespoons (½ stick) unsalted butter

3 garlic cloves, minced

Leaves from 4 sprigs fresh thyme, finely chopped

1 pound cremini mushrooms, sliced

6 (10-inch) flour tortillas

4 cups shredded Monterey Jack cheese

Quesadillas are as easy to make as a grilled cheese sandwich, and these have the bonus of cremini mushrooms. Creminis have a deep earthiness that's far more complex than everyday white button mushrooms, and the fresh thyme amps up the flavor even more. As for the cheese, Monterey Jack happens to be my son Fausto's favorite, but a good Oaxaca or Chihuahua cheese would be excellent here, as well. This is a no-brainer for entertaining but also one of my go-tos for weeknight dinners! I actually love dipping this quesadilla in bean soup (like the one on the opposite page).

Melt the butter in a saucepan over medium-high heat. Add the garlic and thyme leaves and cook until the garlic is fragrant, 2 to 3 minutes. Add the mushrooms and cook, stirring occasionally with a wooden spoon, until the mushrooms are golden brown, 8 to 10 minutes. Remove from the heat and set aside.

Heat a skillet over low heat. Add a tortilla and cook for about 2 minutes, then flip it over. Sprinkle about one-third of the cheese on the tortilla, followed by about one-third of the mushrooms. Cover with another tortilla and cook for about 4 minutes, until the cheese has melted. Flip the quesadilla over and cook for about 3 more minutes, or until the tortilla starts to turn golden and the cheese has completely melted. Transfer to a cutting board and cut into quarters. Repeat with the remaining cheese, mushrooms, and tortillas. Transfer to a platter and serve warm.

CHIPOTLE DEVILED EGGS

MAKES 24 DEVILED EGGS

12 hard-boiled large eggs

⅓ cup mayonnaise

1 tablespoon finely chopped canned chipotle chiles in adobo sauce

1 teaspoon Dijon mustard

Kosher salt and freshly ground black pepper

Chipotle powder, for garnish

Edible flowers (optional), for garnish

2 tablespoons finely chopped fresh chives, for garnish

Deviled eggs are a staple at my get-togethers because they're a good, hearty option for vegetarians. I've learned a few things from serving these over the years: Make life easy by not using super-fresh eggs from the farmers' market; they're harder to peel. Also, prep the eggs a day ahead so you don't have that sulfur smell invading your party. Halve the eggs and fill them just before serving. I add smoky chipotle chile to the filling, then sprinkle them with chipotle powder instead of the usual paprika, and I'm telling you, people go nuts for them. If you don't like chipotle, you can always swap in harissa . . . but then speak to someone, because who doesn't like chipotle?

Peel the eggs and slice them in half lengthwise. Scoop out the yolks and transfer to a medium bowl. Mash the yolks with a fork. Add the mayonnaise, chopped chipotles, and mustard. Mix until smooth, then season to taste with salt and pepper. Spoon or pipe the filling into the egg whites. Cover and refrigerate until ready to serve, at least 2 hours. Transfer to a platter, sprinkle with chipotle powder, the edible flowers, and the chopped chives, and serve.

SMOKED OYSTER CHEESE BALL

SERVES 6 TO 8

2 (8-ounce) packages cream cheese, at room temperature

2 (3-ounce) cans smoked oysters, drained and finely chopped

¼ cup freshly squeezed lemon juice (from 1½ lemons)

1 tablespoon Worcestershire sauce

1½ teaspoons Tabasco sauce

1 teaspoon soy sauce

½ teaspoon garlic powder

Kosher salt and freshly ground black pepper

Finely chopped fresh chives, for coating

Crackers or baguette toasts, for serving

When I was growing up, my father was kind of obsessed with anything canned. You'd think we were eating *chilaquiles* all day at my house, but in reality, his predinner ritual was to crack open a can of something to snack on with saltines and a cocktail. Canned oysters, sardines, clams . . . even asparagus. Naturally, we'd sit there with him and nosh on whatever he had chosen for the evening. So when I was first confronted with an oyster cheese ball at a baby shower, I was flooded with nostalgia. After one bite, I fell in love. Serve the cheese ball with baguette toasts or any mild-flavored crackers.

Combine the cream cheese, oysters, lemon juice, Worcestershire, Tabasco, soy sauce, and garlic powder in a medium bowl. Mix until well combined. Season to taste with salt and pepper. Cover and refrigerate for about 1 hour.

Using your hands, shape the mixture into a ball. Place the ball on a platter and cover with plastic wrap. Refrigerate for 3 hours or up to overnight.

Place the chopped chives on a plate. Roll the cheese ball in the chives to coat all over. Return the cheese ball to the platter. Alternatively, for a looser texture, mound the cheese mixture onto a plate and sprinkle with the chives. Serve with crackers or baguette toasts.

CLAM and ONION DIP

MAKES ABOUT 3 CUPS

3 tablespoons olive oil

½ yellow onion, finely chopped

1 tablespoon balsamic vinegar

1 (6.5-ounce) can chopped clams, drained

1½ cups sour cream

4 ounces cream cheese, at room temperature

2 tablespoons Worcestershire sauce

Kosher salt and freshly ground black pepper

Potato chips, for serving

Take those dusty clam cans out of the pantry and give them new life. (I mean, be sure to check the expiration date, but don't those things last forever?) I could seriously just spread this dip on a baguette and eat it like a sandwich, but that would be weird, so I serve it as an appetizer with sturdy potato chips. Crusty bread or crackers are also great accompaniments . . . as well as a little champagne!

Heat the olive oil in a small saucepan over medium-high heat. Add the onion and cook, stirring, until translucent, about 3 minutes. Add the vinegar and cook, stirring, until it reduces to the consistency of honey, about 3 minutes. Remove from the heat.

Combine the clams, sour cream, cream cheese, and Worcestershire in a medium bowl. Stir to combine, then stir in the onion. Season to taste with salt and pepper. Transfer to your favorite bowl, serve with potato chips, and enjoy!

PARMESAN SCALLOPS

MAKES 16 SCALLOPS

5 tablespoons unsalted butter, melted and cooled

¼ cup freshly squeezed lime juice (from 2 or 3 limes)

1 large shallot, minced

16 sea scallops

1 cup grated Parmesan cheese

Chopped fresh cilantro leaves, for garnish

SPECIAL EQUIPMENT:

16 natural king scallop baking shells (available from Amazon)

I never turn down an invitation to my friend Katia's parties because she always makes the most amazing Peruvian food, and her daughter, Isabella, is a delight. I fell especially hard for these scallops baked with lime butter, then topped with nutty, melted Parmesan cheese. It's a simple dish with a huge punch of flavor. The only thing you need to do in advance is get baking shells (I got mine from Amazon). They're natural sea shells that you can heat over and over again for these scallops or other seafood dishes. Just tell your guests not to throw them out, which can happen if you're not watching! I anchor the shells with a layer of extra-coarse Himalayan salt, which I then reuse as a base for other appetizers that come in a vessel. Without the salt, the shells slide all over the place!

Preheat the oven to 400°F. Arrange the scallop shells on a rimmed baking sheet.

Stir together the butter, lime juice, and shallot in a small bowl.

Place 1 scallop on each baking shell and top the scallops with 1 tablespoon of the lime butter each, then sprinkle each with 1 tablespoon of the cheese. Bake for 10 to 12 minutes, until the scallops are cooked through and the cheese is golden brown. Garnish with chopped cilantro and serve immediately.

SMOKED SALMON TERRINE

SERVES 6 TO 8

CREPES

¾ cup whole milk

2 large eggs

1 large egg yolk

½ cup all-purpose flour

3 tablespoons unsalted butter, melted and cooled

½ teaspoon kosher salt

Vegetable oil or nonstick cooking spray, for greasing

TERRINE

2 (8-ounce) packages cream cheese, at room temperature

¼ cup freshly squeezed lemon juice (from 1½ lemons)

1 tablespoon finely chopped fresh dill

Kosher salt and freshly ground black pepper

Vegetable oil or nonstick cooking spray, for greasing

16 ounces thinly sliced smoked salmon

1 lemon, thinly sliced, for garnish

1 tablespoon finely chopped fresh chives, for garnish

This is another app that looks super impressive but is so simple to prepare. Make it one day ahead to give the terrine a chance to set. I layer the terrine with crepes, which I DIY at home, but I won't judge if you choose to buy them. I've actually seen giant square crepes at the market that would be perfect for this dish. You can serve the terrine whole on a platter and let guests cut it themselves, or serve slices alongside a simple arugula salad for an elegant brunch or lunch.

FOR THE CREPES, place the milk, eggs, egg yolk, flour, melted butter, and salt in a blender and blend until smooth. Let the batter stand for 30 minutes to allow any bubbles to settle.

Heat an 8-inch nonstick skillet over medium-high heat. Brush the pan with oil (or spray with cooking spray). Add a scant ¼ cup of the batter to the skillet and immediately rotate the pan to evenly coat the bottom. Cook until the crepe is golden on the bottom, 30 to 45 seconds. Flip the crepe over with a spatula and cook for 30 seconds more. Transfer to a plate and repeat with the remaining batter. Let cool, then slice each crepe into quarters.

FOR THE TERRINE, place the cream cheese, lemon juice, and dill in a food processor and process until smooth. Season to taste with salt and pepper. Set aside.

Grease an 8 x 4-inch loaf pan with oil or spray with cooking spray. Line the bottom and sides with plastic wrap, leaving a 2-inch overhang on the long sides. Cover the base of the pan with a layer of the smoked salmon. Using a rubber spatula, spread ¼ cup of the cream cheese mixture evenly over the layer of salmon. Top with two pieces of crepe, making sure to cover the salmon. Repeat the layers, finishing with the salmon. Fold the overhanging plastic wrap over the top. Press down gently and refrigerate for 2 hours or until the cream cheese sets.

Just before serving, turn the terrine out onto a platter and discard the plastic wrap. Top with the lemon slices and chopped chives and serve.

OYSTER SHOOTERS

MAKES 8 SHOOTERS

¼ cup vodka, chilled

½ cup ponzu sauce (Japanese citrus soy sauce)

Pinch wasabi powder

8 medium-size oysters, such as Blue Points, freshly shucked

4 teaspoons caviar

2 teaspoons tobikko (flying fish roe)

2 tablespoons finely chopped fresh chives

2 teaspoons grated lime zest

SPECIAL EQUIPMENT:

8 shot glasses, chilled

I was sure the best oyster shooter I'd ever had was in Baja, but that title now goes to the one I tried at a little restaurant called Mala in Lahaina, Hawaii. My brother-in-law Raymundo has actually shown up at my house with all the ingredients to make these shooters for parties, and when he does, I have to admit, it's the appetizer that disappears the quickest! Throw back the shot glass, and you're hit with all the Asian flavors you love, plus a hint of fresh, icy vodka. Then you finish with pops of caviar and *tobikko* (flying fish roe). Playful and fun, these shooters will take your guests on a thrill ride.

Pour 1½ teaspoons of the vodka into each shot glass. Combine the ponzu sauce and wasabi powder in a liquid measuring cup. Divide the sauce evenly among the glasses, about 1 tablespoon per glass. Add 1 oyster to each glass and divide the caviar, tobikko, chives, and lime zest evenly on top of the oysters. Serve immediately.

SUSHI CAKE with SERRANO-PONZU SAUCE

SERVES 8 TO 10

Nonstick cooking spray

SERRANO-PONZU SAUCE

1 cup ponzu sauce (Japanese citrus soy sauce)

1 fresh serrano chile, thinly sliced

¼ cup freshly squeezed lime juice (from 2 or 3 limes)

3 scallions, chopped

SUSHI CAKE

2 cups steamed sushi rice, still warm

½ cup rice vinegar

2 tablespoons granulated sugar

2 teaspoons kosher salt

4 ounces cream cheese, at room temperature

½ cup mayonnaise

3 tablespoons sriracha

2 tablespoons freshly squeezed lime juice

16 ounces lump crabmeat, picked over to remove any shell

Kosher salt and freshly ground black pepper

1 avocado, sliced

2 large carrots, grated

1 medium cucumber, peeled, grated, and drained

Black sesame seeds, for garnish

White sesame seeds, for garnish

Fresh chives, for garnish

SPECIAL EQUIPMENT:

12-cup Bundt pan

When I proposed this recipe to my editor, he was like, "Um, this doesn't belong in your book." So I had to explain why I wanted to include it. We Mexicans are known for our ingenious ideas and problem-solving capabilities. So how do you prepare sushi for a bunch of people without making a gazillion individual rolls? You layer the ingredients in a Bundt pan. Now, I understand sushi isn't what comes to mind when you think of Mexico, but you will find some version of this dish at a lot of gatherings south of the border! In Tijuana, it's an absolute favorite at parties and showers. We just like the ease of constructing food in Bundt pans. Try it and surprise your guests!

Line the Bundt pan with plastic wrap, leaving 2 inches of overhang all around. Spray with cooking spray and set the pan aside.

FOR THE SERRANO-PONZU SAUCE, combine the ponzu sauce, serrano, lime juice, and scallions in a medium bowl and refrigerate until ready to serve.

FOR THE SUSHI CAKE, combine the rice, vinegar, sugar, and salt in a large bowl and mix to combine. Cover and let cool for at least 15 minutes. The rice should be completely cool before you assemble the cake.

Combine the cream cheese, mayonnaise, sriracha, and lime juice in a large bowl. Mix until smooth. Fold in the crabmeat and season to taste with salt and pepper.

To assemble the sushi cake, place ¾ cup of the cooled rice in the bottom of the prepared Bundt pan, pressing the rice firmly all around to create an even layer. Top with half the avocado slices and all the shredded carrots, spicy crab, and cucumber. Season lightly with salt and pepper. Top with the remaining avocado slices and remaining 1¼ cups rice. Cover with plastic wrap and refrigerate for at least 2½ hours, or until the cake is firm.

Carefully unmold the sushi cake onto a serving platter and discard the plastic wrap. Sprinkle the black and white sesame seeds on top of the cake, garnish with chives, then slice and serve with the chilled serrano-ponzu sauce.

SMOKED SALMON and SPINACH ROULADE

SERVES 6

Nonstick cooking spray

12 ounces chopped frozen spinach, thawed and drained

4 large eggs, separated

⅓ cup grated Parmesan cheese

½ cup grated Gruyère cheese

Kosher salt and freshly ground black pepper

1 (8-ounce) package cream cheese, at room temperature

2 tablespoons finely chopped fresh chives

8 ounces thinly sliced smoked salmon

My aunt Marcela graduated from the California Culinary Academy, and she dated a very handsome Italian chef (who was also her professor—gasp!). He would visit us in Tijuana and prepare the most incredible meals with my grandfather and aunt. I was so young, all I remember is a salmon roulade she made once from a recipe in a cookbook—it blew my mind. I've searched high and low for that recipe with no luck, so I created this version from my taste memory. Spinach, Gruyère, salmon, and cream cheese . . . I mean, what's not to love?

―――――――――――――

Preheat the oven to 400°F. Spray an 8 x 12-inch glass baking dish with cooking spray and line it with parchment paper.

Squeeze as much liquid out of the spinach as possible with a clean kitchen towel or paper towels. Set aside.

Whisk the egg yolks in a medium bowl. Add the spinach, Parmesan, and Gruyère and mix to combine. Season with salt and pepper.

Using a handheld mixer, whisk the egg whites in a large bowl on high speed until stiff peaks form. Using a rubber spatula, fold the egg whites into the spinach mixture. Pour into the prepared baking dish and spread evenly. Bake for 15 minutes, until set and light golden brown.

recipe continues

Turn out the roulade onto a large sheet of parchment paper. Peel off and discard the parchment lining from the baking dish. Drape the roulade along the length of a clean glass bottle (this will make it pliable for rolling) and let cool.

Meanwhile, mix the cream cheese and chopped chives in a small bowl until smooth. Season to taste with salt and pepper.

Return the cooled roulade to the sheet of parchment paper and spread it with the cream cheese mixture. Top with an even layer of the smoked salmon. Starting from one short end, roll up the roulade into a tight log. Cover with plastic wrap and refrigerate until ready to serve. Slice the roulade crosswise, transfer to a platter, and serve.

PICADILLO LETTUCE CUPS

SERVES 6 TO 8

1 tablespoon olive oil

8 ounces ground beef

Kosher salt and freshly ground black pepper

2 large carrots, finely chopped

1 large zucchini, finely chopped

½ onion, finely chopped

½ cup canned tomato puree or sauce

1 head butter lettuce, separated into leaves, for serving

Avocado slices, for serving

Lime wedges, for serving

Picadillo (ground meat cooked with vegetables and tomato puree) is great in tortillas and on any kind of bun. But to be honest, I love the contrast of crisp, cold lettuce wraps with the warm and hearty beef filling. In terms of toppings, keep it simple or go full-on taco bar: Set out avocado slices, fresh salsa, pickled jalapeños, lime wedges, or pickled onions (there are some good ones on page 142). Pretty much anything goes!

Heat the olive oil in a heavy sauté pan over medium-high heat. Add the ground beef and cook, stirring, until browned, about 6 minutes. Season to taste with salt and pepper. Add the carrots, zucchini, and onion and cook, stirring, until the vegetables soften, 2 to 3 minutes. Season to taste with salt and pepper. Add the tomato puree and simmer, stirring occasionally, until bright red, about 10 minutes. Season to taste with salt and pepper. Remove from the heat and let cool to room temperature.

Serve the picadillo in the lettuce cups immediately with the avocado slices and lime wedges.

SWEET-AND-SPICY WINGS

SERVES 10 TO 12

¾ cup (1½ sticks) unsalted butter

2 cups honey

1 cup chopped pecans

¼ cup white vinegar

¼ cup Worcestershire sauce

3 tablespoons ancho chile powder

1 tablespoon garlic powder

Kosher salt and freshly ground black pepper

4 pounds chicken wings

This recipe is a tweaked version of my dad's favorite wings. I should also admit that I gave my dear friend Bobby Flay a really hard time about his obsession with combining honey with ancho chiles. Yet here I am, making ancho-honey wings—because you know what? It works. So I'm sorry, Bobby! Love ya! Serve these sticky wings at your game-day parties, whether it's the Super Bowl or the FIFA World Cup. I think Bobby would approve.

Preheat the oven to 350°F.

Melt the butter in a small saucepan over medium-low heat. Stir in the honey and cook until the mixture bubbles, about 3 minutes. Remove from the heat and stir in the pecans, vinegar, Worcestershire, ancho chile powder, and garlic powder. Season the glaze to taste with salt and pepper.

Arrange the wings on a rimmed baking sheet and brush them with the glaze. Bake until the chicken is cooked through, about 25 minutes, basting once halfway through the baking time. Transfer the wings to a serving platter and serve hot.

TURKEY COCKTAIL MEATBALLS with APRICOT- CHIPOTLE GLAZE

MAKES 30 COCKTAIL-SIZE MEATBALLS

Vegetable oil, for greasing

1 pound lean ground turkey

2 large eggs, beaten

½ cup panko bread crumbs

1 tablespoon chopped fresh parsley, plus more for garnish

2 teaspoons Worcestershire sauce

½ teaspoon garlic powder

½ teaspoon onion powder

½ teaspoon kosher salt, plus more for the glaze

¼ teaspoon freshly ground black pepper, plus more for the glaze

½ cup apricot jam

1 tablespoon adobo sauce (from a can of chipotle chiles in adobo)

1 tablespoon apple cider vinegar

Nobody can pass up little cocktail meatballs at a party. They practically beg to be eaten—especially these juicy ones made with ground turkey. The secret is to baste them while baking to create that sticky-sweet glaze and trap in moisture. No toothpicks for serving? No sweat. Do what I do and look for nature's toothpicks outside. Rosemary sprigs work great, but any twig that's thoroughly scrubbed and washed will work.

Preheat the oven to 375°F. Grease a rimmed baking sheet with vegetable oil.

Combine the ground turkey, eggs, panko, parsley, Worcestershire, garlic powder, onion powder, salt, and pepper in a large bowl. Mix with your hands until incorporated. Roll the mixture into 1-inch meatballs and transfer them to the prepared baking sheet.

Combine the apricot jam, adobo sauce, and vinegar in a small bowl and stir well. Season to taste with salt and pepper. Using a pastry brush, generously coat the meatballs, reserving some glaze. Roast the meatballs until firm and cooked through, about 15 minutes. Remove from the oven and turn on the broiler. Brush the meatballs with the reserved glaze and broil until the glaze is shiny and caramelized, about 12 minutes. Transfer to a platter, sprinkle with chopped parsley, and serve immediately with toothpicks.

FRIED CHICKEN and CHORIZO WAFFLES

MAKES 16 FRIED DRUMETTES AND 16 WAFFLE WEDGES

FRIED CHICKEN

3 cups well-shaken buttermilk

16 chicken drumettes, about 2 pounds

1½ cups all-purpose flour

1½ teaspoons kosher salt

½ teaspoon garlic powder

Freshly ground black pepper

━━━

CHORIZO WAFFLES

Nonstick cooking spray

1 cup all-purpose flour

1 teaspoon baking powder

½ teaspoon kosher salt

¼ teaspoon baking soda

1 cup well-shaken buttermilk

6 tablespoons (¾ stick) unsalted butter, melted and cooled

1 large egg

8 ounces fresh pork chorizo, casings removed, cooked until crispy and drained well on paper towels (see Note, page 139)

━━━

2 cups vegetable oil, for frying

Pure maple syrup, for serving

Minced green onions, for garnish

━━━

SPECIAL EQUIPMENT:

8-inch round waffle iron, instant-read thermometer

The great thing about the fried chicken here is that I use drumettes (the meatiest part of the wing). That way, you get smaller pieces of chicken, which yields a higher ratio of coating to meat. After all, the crispy, crunchy breading is the best part! You can absolutely use any fried chicken recipe you like or, heck, even buy it! All you really HAVE to make from scratch are the chorizo waffles. Be sure to render all the fat from the chorizo and drain the crispy bits even more on paper towels; otherwise, the excess fat in the batter won't let the waffles set properly. By the way, the waffles are also a delicious breakfast all by themselves, served with plenty of butter and maple syrup!

FOR THE CHICKEN, combine the buttermilk and chicken in a large, shallow nonreactive dish. Cover and refrigerate for at least 3 hours or up to overnight.

Combine the flour, salt, and garlic powder in a large resealable plastic bag, season with pepper, and set aside.

FOR THE CHORIZO WAFFLES, preheat the oven to 250°F. Spray the waffle iron with cooking spray and preheat it.

Sift the flour, baking powder, salt, and baking soda into a medium bowl.

Whisk together the buttermilk, melted butter, and egg in another medium bowl. Add the wet ingredients to the dry ingredients and whisk until smooth. (The batter will be thick.) Fold in the cooked chorizo.

Spoon ¾ cup of the batter into the waffle iron and spread evenly. Cook according to the manufacturer's instructions until golden brown. Transfer the waffle to a baking sheet and keep warm in the middle of the oven. Repeat with the remaining batter, but do not respray the waffle iron.

Pour the vegetable oil into a large heavy skillet and heat over medium-high heat until the oil registers 350°F on the deep-fry thermometer.

MEANWHILE, REMOVE A FEW OF THE CHICKEN DRUMETTES from the buttermilk and transfer them to the bag of seasoned flour. Shake to coat, then dust off the excess coating and set on a plate. Repeat with the remaining chicken. Discard the remaining buttermilk and seasoned flour.

Reduce the heat under the oil to medium. Add the chicken to the hot oil, a few pieces at a time, and fry, turning occasionally, until crispy and golden and the internal temperature registers 165°F on an instant-read thermometer, 10 to 12 minutes. Transfer the fried chicken to a rack and set aside until ready to serve. Repeat to fry the remaining chicken.

TO ASSEMBLE, cut each chorizo waffle into 4 wedges. Drizzle 1 wedge with maple syrup, top with green onions, then transfer to a platter and serve right away with a drumette.

note

Be sure to use Mexican chorizo, which is made with fresh ground pork. Spanish chorizo, on the other hand, is cured and drier in consistency, like salami.

SLOW COOKER LAMB MINI TACOS

MAKES 16 TACOS

1 teaspoon dried rosemary

1 teaspoon dried oregano

1 tablespoon kosher salt, or to taste

2 teaspoons freshly ground black pepper

½ cup olive oil

1 (4½-pound) whole semi-boneless leg of lamb

3 large shallots, sliced

5 garlic cloves

4 cups lager beer (buy three 12-ounce bottles and you can drink the leftovers)

16 corn tortillas, warmed

Roasted Tomatillo and Green Apple Salsa (page 153)

Lime wedges, for serving

Taco parties are my absolute fave because they're low-maintenance and the food is always a crowd-pleaser. I can make most of the fillings ahead of time, buy some of the toppings already prepared, then just set everything out for guests to help themselves. Sometimes I go for something different and fun for the taco bar, like this beer-braised lamb that becomes fall-apart tender in the slow cooker. It has a distinct flavor that I find exquisite, but feel free to swap the lamb out for beef chuck instead. As for the roasted tomatillo and green apple salsa, it's fabulous with these little tacos but also excellent as a dip for warm, homemade tortilla chips!

Combine the rosemary, oregano, salt, pepper, and olive oil in a small bowl and stir to combine. Rub the mixture all over the lamb and transfer to a slow cooker. Add the shallots and garlic and pour the beer around the lamb. Cover and cook on High for 5 hours, or until the lamb is fork-tender. With the slow cooker still on High, remove the lamb and transfer it to a platter. Shred the meat, discarding any bones. Return the shredded lamb to the slow cooker and cook for 1 hour more.

Preheat the broiler.

Turn off the slow cooker and, using tongs, transfer the lamb to a large cast-iron skillet. Reserve the juices in the slow cooker for serving.

Broil the lamb until crispy, 7 minutes. Pour the reserved juices over the lamb and serve immediately with the tortillas, Roasted Tomatillo and Green Apple Salsa, and lime wedges.

SLOW COOKER COCHINITA PIBIL TOSTADAS

SERVES 8 TO 10

COCHINITA PIBIL

1½ cups freshly squeezed orange juice (from 3 to 6 oranges)

5 garlic cloves

2 tablespoons achiote paste (see Note. page 144)

2 tablespoons white vinegar

1½ teaspoons dried Mexican oregano

Kosher salt

2½ pounds boneless pork butt, cut into 2-inch cubes

½ medium onion

2 bay leaves

2 cinnamon sticks

1 teaspoon whole black peppercorns

3 whole cloves

———

PICKLED RED ONIONS

1 red onion, quartered and sliced into 1-inch-wide strips

1 habanero chile, stemmed, seeded, deveined, and finely chopped

½ cup freshly squeezed lime juice (from 5 limes)

¼ cup red wine vinegar

¼ cup extra-virgin olive oil

1 tablespoon crumbled dried Mexican oregano

1½ teaspoons kosher salt

———

FOR SERVING

8 corn tortillas

Vegetable oil, for brushing

2 avocados, thinly sliced

Caramelized Hibiscus Salsa (page 152)

———

Unless you want to dig a barbecue pit in your backyard, using a slow cooker for this Yucatán-style roasted pork is the best way to achieve the tenderest meat. Achiote paste (ground annatto seeds compressed into a brick) gives the shredded pork its unique, earthy flavor but it also has a bitter note and grittiness that can only be overcome with a long cook time. That's why the slow cooker is a godsend. Achiote paste is available in East Indian markets, Latin markets, and some supermarkets, as well as online.

note

Achiote paste comes from ground achiote seeds, also known as annatto seeds. The paste not only adds musky, earthy flavor to a dish, but also gives it a brick-red color. In Mexico, it is often used by cooks in the Yucatán, where it is mixed with the bright citrus juice of bitter oranges or limes and then spread on fish for grilling or pork for roasting.

FOR THE COCHINITA PIBIL, combine the orange juice, garlic, achiote, vinegar, and oregano in a blender and blend until smooth. Season to taste with salt.

Combine the pork, onion, bay leaves, cinnamon sticks, peppercorns, and cloves in a slow cooker. Cover with the orange-achiote mixture. Cover and cook on High for about 5 hours, or until the pork is tender and falls apart when pulled with a fork.

MEANWHILE, FOR THE PICKLED RED ONIONS, combine the onion, habanero, lime juice, vinegar, olive oil, oregano, and salt in a medium bowl and mix to combine. Refrigerate for at least 2 hours or up to overnight.

About 40 minutes before you're ready to serve, preheat the oven to 350°F.

Lightly brush each tortilla with vegetable oil and place them on a baking sheet. Bake for about 20 minutes, or until crispy. Let the tostadas cool slightly. If desired, break them into chip-size pieces (about 3 inches). Set the tostadas aside until ready to serve.

When the pork is done, transfer it to a large baking dish and let cool slightly. Shred the pork with two forks and discard any excess fat. Pour the cooking juices from the slow cooker over the shredded pork and stir to combine.

Transfer the cochinita pibil to a serving dish and serve with the tostadas, pickled onions, sliced avocado, and Caramelized Hibiscus Salsa.

SANDWICHON
(SANDWICH CAKE)

SERVES 8

4 (6-ounce) cans tuna, drained (water- or oil-packed, your choice)

½ cup plus 5 tablespoons mayonnaise

1 tablespoon mustard

1 (11-ounce) can pickled whole jalapeños, drained, ¼ cup of the liquid reserved

3 tablespoons adobo sauce (from a can of chipotle chiles in adobo)

3½ (8-ounce) packages cream cheese, at room temperature

Kosher salt and freshly ground pepper

1½ cups diced ham

1 tablespoon extra-virgin olive oil

24 slices white bread, crusts removed and discarded, sliced in half

14 slices American cheese

¼ cup evaporated milk

Chopped mixed fresh herbs, very thinly sliced zucchini or radishes, or olives and roasted bell peppers, for garnish (optional)

Just like with the sushi cake on page 125, my editor was very confused about this particular recipe appearing in this here book. But, Justin, listen, this savory cake is a staple at first communions, baby showers, baptisms, and even birthday parties all across Mexico. If you head to Pinterest and search for "sandwich cake," you'll find plenty of pins that look like the original and totally Swedish *smörgåstårta*. But Pinterest also has a massive number of recipes in Spanish, so if you search for "sandwichon," you'll find hundreds of pins for this variation on the famous Swedish dish. Instead of fancy ingredients like caviar, smoked fish, cold cuts, or liver pâté, *sandwichon* fillings include chicken salad, tuna salad, and my very personal favorite: ham, mayo, and a bit of cream cheese blended with plenty of salt. I know it may sound weird. When I've blogged about it, my American followers (except for a few in Texas) don't really recognize it. But my Mexican or Hispanic followers? They go INSANE, because *sandwichon* takes them to a very happy place in their childhood. But don't think of this nostalgic party dish as a thing of the past. It's alive and well and at a *primera* communion near you . . .

Line a 9-inch springform pan with plastic wrap and set aside.

Combine the tuna, 3 tablespoons of the mayonnaise, the mustard, pickling liquid, adobo sauce, and ½ package of the cream cheese in a medium bowl. Mix to combine and season to taste with salt and pepper. Cover and refrigerate until ready to assemble the sandwichon.

Combine ½ cup of the mayonnaise, the ham, and the olive oil in a food processor. Process until smooth. Season to taste with salt.

Cover the bottom of the prepared pan with 12 pieces of the bread, overlapping them, if necessary, to make sure there are no gaps between the pieces. Spread half the tuna salad on top of the bread layer. Cover the tuna layer with 7 slices of the cheese. Slice 2 of the pickled jalapeños lengthwise and scatter half the slices over the cheese layer. Cover the cheese layer with 12 more pieces of bread. Spread the ham mixture on top of the bread layer. Cover the ham layer with 12 more pieces of bread. Spread the remaining tuna salad on the bread layer and top with the remaining slices of cheese. Scatter the remaining jalapeño slices over the cheese. Finish the sandwichon with the remaining 12 pieces of bread, again making sure there are no gaps between the pieces (this will help all the layers stay in place). Cover and refrigerate for 2 to 3 hours.

Combine the remaining 3 packages cream cheese, remaining 2 tablespoons mayonnaise, and the evaporated milk in the bowl of a stand mixer fitted with the whisk attachment. Beat until the mixture is smooth and has the consistency of frosting. Season to taste with salt.

Remove the sandwichon from the pan using the plastic wrap. Transfer to a serving platter and discard the plastic wrap. Use a rubber spatula to frost the cake with half the cream cheese mixture (this first layer will be a bit messy). Cover and refrigerate the cake for about 25 minutes, or until the frosting is set. Remove the cake from the refrigerator and spread the remaining cream cheese mixture over the first layer of frosting, making sure it is smooth. Cover and refrigerate for at least 3 hours and up to 2 days before serving.

If desired, sprinkle a mix of chopped fresh herbs over the cake (I like to use basil, chives, and parsley), or decorate the cake with zucchini or radish slices, or olives and roasted red peppers. Slice the sandwichon into wedges and serve.

WHIPPED TRUFFLE and PARMESAN CREAM PUFFS

MAKES 24 PUFFS

PÂTE À CHOUX

1 cup water

½ cup (1 stick) unsalted butter, cubed, at room temperature

1 tablespoon granulated sugar

Large pinch of salt

1 cup all-purpose flour

3 large eggs

Black sesame seeds, for sprinkling

WHIPPED TRUFFLE AND PARMESAN CREAM

1 cup heavy cream

¾ cup grated Parmesan cheese

1 tablespoon truffle oil

1 teaspoon finely chopped fresh thyme

Kosher salt and freshly ground black pepper

Once you master the cream puff, it's really fun to dream up fillings for these little pastry bites. I wanted to offer both a savory option and a sweet option (page 179) to get your imagination rolling. As long as your filling is the right consistency (soft, with just the right touch of firm), you can make any kind of cream puffs you want. Here I go fancy with the flavor of nutty Parmesan and earthy, fragrant truffles. These cream puffs are amazing served with a glass of crisp champagne.

FOR THE PÂTE À CHOUX, preheat the oven to 350°F. Line a baking sheet with parchment paper.

Combine the water, butter, sugar, and salt in a medium saucepan. Cook over medium heat, stirring occasionally, until the water comes to a boil and the butter has completely melted. Add the flour and remove from the heat. Stir with a wooden spoon until the flour absorbs all the liquid and forms a dough. Return the pan to medium heat and cook the dough, stirring, until the dough pulls away from the sides of the pan, 5 to 7 minutes.

Transfer the dough to a bowl and let cool slightly. Add the eggs one at a time, whisking well after each addition. The dough should be glossy and have a pipeable consistency.

Transfer the dough to a pastry bag fitted with a large tip. Pipe about twenty-four 2-inch mounds onto the prepared baking sheet. Sprinkle the mounds with black sesame seeds. Bake for 20 to 25 minutes, until the pastry shells are golden brown on top. Remove from the oven and pierce each shell with a toothpick. Let cool completely.

MEANWHILE, FOR THE TRUFFLE AND PARMESAN CREAM, place the cream in the bowl of a stand mixer fitted with the whisk attachment. Beat on medium speed until soft peaks form, about 3 minutes. Using a rubber spatula, fold in the cheese, truffle oil, and thyme and season to taste with salt and pepper. Transfer the truffle and Parmesan cream to a pastry bag fitted with a medium tip. Pipe the cream into the cooled pastry shells and serve immediately.

PEKING DUCK BURRITOS

MAKES 12 BURRITOS

½ cup hoisin sauce

3 tablespoons adobo sauce (from a can of chipotle chiles in adobo)

12 (8-inch) flour tortillas, warmed (see Note)

3 cups chopped Chinese roast duck (from about one 4-pound duck)

1 cucumber, peeled, cored, and sliced into 2-inch-long strips

4 scallions, sliced into 2-inch-long strips

Leaves from ½ bunch fresh cilantro

More than a recipe, this is where you do some REALLY good research and track down the best authentic Chinese roast duck in town and true Mexican flour tortillas. I actually went on this exact same scavenger hunt years ago when my mom threw me a Chinese-themed baby shower. Other than the fact that every single gathering she ever organized HAD to have a theme, there was absolutely no reason why we were celebrating the upcoming birth of my very Mexican child Fausto wearing qi pao dresses and eating Peking duck. She wasn't completely off track, though. We do have a huge Chinese community in Baja, and you can find much better Chinese food south of the border than in many places in California. Here I use flour tortillas instead of the traditional bun or pancake to wrap the duck. But I have to stress: They have to be real Mexican tortillas. Commercial ones are too thick, hard to roll, and, honestly, don't taste very good. So head to the Mexican market and get you some good ol' lard-based handmade flour tortillas.

Combine the hoisin sauce and adobo sauce in a medium bowl and stir until combined. Set aside.

Place 1 warmed tortilla on a work surface and spread about 1 teaspoon of the adobo-hoisin sauce in the center. Top with ¼ cup of the chopped duck, about 4 cucumber strips, 4 scallion strips, and 3 or 4 cilantro leaves. Roll into a burrito and cut diagonally in half. Repeat with the remaining ingredients. Arrange the burritos on a platter and serve with the remaining adobo-hoisin sauce for dipping.

note

Make sure not to heat the tortillas until crispy because they will break when you roll them.

CARAMELIZED HIBISCUS SALSA

SERVES 4 TO 6

2 cups dried hibiscus flowers
(flor de Jamaica; see page 46)

2 tablespoons extra-virgin
olive oil

1 shallot, finely chopped

½ cup grated
piloncillo (unrefined whole cane
sugar; available at Latin markets)

2 tablespoons water

Kosher salt

This magical salsa came about when I had all the leftover flowers from the Hibiscus Ice Pops recipe (page 46). After steeping, the dried hibiscus flowers become soft and chewy, and have a nice tartness that works beautifully in a salsa. I caramelize them with sugar so the salsa has a delicious, syrupy coating. You can serve the salsa in so many ways: as a filling for a vegan taco, a topping for grilled fish or chicken, mixed into a salad. It's always a huge hit with my Mexican guests because even though they're familiar with hibiscus in *aguas frescas*, seeing it in a savory salsa is totally untraditional and very exciting!

Combine the dried hibiscus flowers and 4 cups water in a large pot and cook over medium heat until the flowers become soft, about 45 minutes. Drain the flowers, reserving the liquid for another use.

Heat the olive oil in a medium pan over medium-high heat. Add the shallot and cook, stirring, until fragrant, about 3 minutes. Add the piloncillo and cook, stirring, until the piloncillo has dissolved completely. Add the 2 tablespoons water and stir until combined. Add the drained hibiscus flowers and cook, stirring occasionally, until caramelized, about 6 minutes, making sure the hibiscus and shallot are completely coated with the piloncillo caramel and the caramel doesn't harden. Season to taste with salt, transfer to a small bowl, and serve.

ROASTED TOMATILLO and GREEN APPLE SALSA

MAKES 4 CUPS

1 pound tomatillos (about 12), husked and rinsed

2 Granny Smith apples, quartered and cored

½ medium white onion

2 jalapeños, stemmed

2 garlic cloves, unpeeled

2 tablespoons extra-virgin olive oil

2 teaspoons kosher salt, plus more for seasoning

1 teaspoon freshly ground black pepper, plus more for seasoning

½ cup chopped fresh cilantro

2 to 3 tablespoons water (optional)

This salsa is like a classic salsa verde but with the surprise addition of sweet-tart Granny Smith apples. It has an applesauce-like consistency, which is ideal for entertaining because it can sit out for a while without separating (the way blended salsas tend to). I love this salsa with tortilla chips, on all types of tacos, or even with enchiladas!

Preheat the oven to 400°F.

Place the tomatillos, apples, onion, jalapeños, and garlic on a rimmed baking sheet. Toss with the olive oil, salt, and pepper. Roast until the tomatillos are softened and slightly charred, about 20 minutes. Remove from the oven and peel the garlic. Let the roasted vegetable mixture cool slightly. Transfer the vegetables and roasted garlic to a blender, add the cilantro, and process until smooth. Add the water, 1 tablespoon at a time, to help blend, if necessary. Season the salsa to taste with salt and pepper, transfer to a serving bowl, and serve.

SHRIMP in ESCABECHE

MAKES 14 TO 16 SIDES

3 tablespoons plus 2 teaspoons kosher salt

2 cups 2-inch cauliflower florets

2 russet potatoes, peeled, cut in half lengthwise, and sliced into ¼-inch-thick half-moons

4 carrots, sliced on an angle

6 jalapeños, seeded, deveined, and sliced lengthwise into strips

1½ cups extra-virgin olive oil

4 garlic cloves, halved

1 red onion, sliced

1 cup white vinegar

15 whole black peppercorns

4 bay leaves

4 teaspoons crumbled dried Mexican oregano

2 pounds shell-on large shrimp (21 to 25 per pound), peeled (tails left on) and deveined

This dish is like the Latin version of pickled shrimp. You basically marinate cooked shrimp in vinegar along with chiles and a bunch of vegetables. This lets all the ingredients maintain a good texture and develop a ton of flavor. Escabeche is fantastic as a main course or side dish served with rice or tostadas. For parties, I like to serve it in shot glasses with toothpicks as passed hors d'oeuvres.

Bring 10 cups water to a boil in a large pot. Season with 1 tablespoon of the salt, add the cauliflower and potatoes, and cook for 5 minutes. Remove from the pot with a slotted spoon and drain in a colander. Add the carrots to the pot and cook for 3 minutes. Remove the carrots with a slotted spoon and transfer to the colander. Add the jalapeños to the pot, cook for 2 minutes, then drain. Transfer all the cooked vegetables to a glass baking dish.

Heat the olive oil in a large heavy sauté pan over medium heat. Add the garlic and cook, stirring, until fragrant, about 4 minutes. Add the onion and cook, stirring, until softened but not browned, about 2 minutes. Remove from the heat. Add a drop or two of the vinegar to the oil in the pan. If it spatters, let the oil cool for a few minutes more and then test it again (repeat until it no longer spatters). When the oil is cool enough, add the remaining vinegar, the peppercorns, bay leaves, oregano, and 2 teaspoons of the salt. Stir to combine. Return the pan to medium heat, bring to a simmer, and cook for 3 minutes. Pour this liquid over the vegetables in the baking dish and toss to combine. Let the vegetables cool to room temperature.

recipe continues

Meanwhile, bring a medium pot of water to a boil. Add the remaining 2 tablespoons salt and the shrimp. Reduce the heat to low and cook, uncovered, for about 5 minutes. Drain well, then stir the shrimp into the pickled veggie mixture. Cover with plastic wrap and refrigerate overnight. Transfer to a platter and serve family-style or in shot glasses with toothpicks.

TOMATILLO PANZANELLA

SERVES 6 TO 8

4 cups cubed sourdough bread

2 teaspoons dried basil

¾ cup extra-virgin olive oil

¼ cup freshly squeezed lemon juice

1 tablespoon Dijon mustard

1 garlic clove, minced

1 tablespoon honey

1 tablespoon white wine vinegar

Kosher salt and freshly ground black pepper

5 heirloom tomatoes, cored and chopped into medium pieces

5 tomatillos, quartered

10 ounces panela cheese, cut into 1-inch cubes

2 cups crumbled chicharrón (pork cracklings)

½ small red onion, thinly sliced

15 fresh basil leaves, coarsely chopped, plus more whole leaves for garnish

Panzanella is a classic Italian salad of tomato and bread. Here I give it a Cal-Mex twist with tangy tomatillos and sourdough bread. I also make my version extra hearty by adding cubes of creamy, mild panela cheese and crumbled *chicharrón* (pork cracklings) for extra crunch. This salad is a terrific option for buffets because the bread soaks up all the delicious juices from the tomatoes and tomatillos as it sits.

Preheat the oven to 325°F.

Place the bread cubes in a large bowl. Add the dried basil and ¼ cup of the olive oil and toss to combine. Transfer the bread cubes to a rimmed baking sheet. Bake for 25 to 30 minutes, stirring occasionally, until browned. Remove from the oven and let the croutons cool to room temperature.

Combine the remaining ½ cup olive oil, the lemon juice, mustard, garlic, honey, and vinegar in a large bowl. Whisk until combined. Season with salt and pepper to taste. Add the tomatoes, tomatillos, panela cheese, chicharrón, onion, chopped basil, and croutons. Toss with the vinaigrette. Season to taste with salt and pepper. Transfer the salad to a large platter, garnish with whole basil leaves, and serve.

BEEF SLIDERS with CHIPOTLE SPECIAL SAUCE

MAKES 10 SLIDERS

CHIPOTLE SPECIAL SAUCE

6 tablespoons mayonnaise

3 tablespoons ketchup

1 tablespoon adobo sauce (from a can of chipotle chiles in adobo)

2 teaspoons diced pickled jalapeños

2 teaspoons prepared horseradish

1 shallot, minced

2 teaspoons chopped fresh parsley

Kosher salt and freshly ground black pepper

———

BEEF PATTIES

1 pound ground beef

1 teaspoon garlic powder

1 teaspoon onion powder

1 tablespoon kosher salt

1 teaspoon Worcestershire sauce

½ teaspoon freshly ground black pepper

Canola oil, for frying

———

10 slices sharp cheddar cheese (about 2x2 inches)

2 tablespoons unsalted butter

10 mini brioche buns

2 Bibb lettuce leaves, cut into 5 pieces each

10 pickled jalapeño strips

10 slices pickled carrots (from a can of pickled jalapeños)

———

SPECIAL EQUIPMENT:

10 bamboo picks

———

Sliders are awesome for parties because they're small enough for people who don't want to commit to a full-size burger. What makes these extra good is the special sauce that's smoky from chipotles and tangy-hot from pickled jalapeños. Serve the sauce on the side for the kiddos. They love these mini burgers sized just for them!

FOR THE CHIPOTLE SPECIAL SAUCE, stir together the mayonnaise, ketchup, adobo sauce, jalapeños, horseradish, shallot, and parsley in a small bowl. Season to taste with salt and pepper and set aside.

FOR THE BEEF PATTIES, mix the ground beef, garlic powder, onion powder, salt, Worcestershire, and pepper in a large bowl. Form the meat mixture into ten 2-inch patties.

Heat a cast-iron skillet over medium-high heat. Add enough canola oil to coat the bottom of the pan and heat until the oil is smoking. Add the patties and cook until seared on both sides and heavily caramelized, 4 to 6 minutes for medium-rare. Top each patty with a slice of cheese. Transfer the patties to a plate. Wipe out the pan, add the butter, and melt over low heat. Add the buns cut-side down and toast them in the butter. Remove from the heat.

Spread the chipotle special sauce on both cut sides of each bun. Place a patty and a piece of lettuce on each bun and close the sliders. Top each slider with a pickled jalapeño strip and a pickled carrot slice, securing them with a bamboo pick. Serve right away.

CHICKEN CHOPPED SALAD

MAKES 6 CUPS (SERVES 12)

2 tablespoons apple cider vinegar

2 tablespoons freshly squeezed lime juice

2 teaspoons sea salt

1 teaspoon dried Mexican oregano

1 teaspoon brown sugar

1 teaspoon freshly ground black pepper

½ cup extra-virgin olive oil

1½ pounds chicken breasts (about 2)

3 ripe avocados (about 2 pounds), pitted, peeled, and cut into large chunks

1 (14-ounce) can hearts of palm, drained, rinsed, and sliced into ½-inch-thick rounds

1 cup fresh corn kernels (from about 1 ear)

10½ ounces cherry tomatoes (about 2 cups), halved

2 tablespoons minced shallot

¼ cup pepitas (hulled pumpkin seeds), toasted

Vegetable oil, for greasing

12 corn husks, for serving

This isn't the creamy type of chicken salad laden with mayo. It's a lighter, brighter version tossed in a tangy lime vinaigrette. I add hearts of palm, fresh corn, and cherry tomatoes, then serve it all in a corn husk so everyone can *ooh* and *ahh* over the presentation. You could also make mini sandwiches with a baguette for a larger platter. Either way, a bowl of pickled jalapeños to serve alongside is a must. From a can is totally fine! Look for the ones that have lots of sliced carrots—those are the best!

Combine the vinegar, lime juice, salt, oregano, sugar, and pepper in a small bowl. While whisking, pour in the olive oil in a slow, steady stream and whisk until emulsified.

Pour half the vinaigrette into a resealable plastic bag and add the chicken. Seal the bag and marinate at room temperature for 20 minutes or in the refrigerator for up to 2 hours. Set the remaining vinaigrette aside.

Gently mix the avocados, hearts of palm, corn, cherry tomatoes, and shallot in a medium bowl. Add the remaining vinaigrette and toss. Sprinkle with the pepitas and set aside.

Grease a grill pan with vegetable oil and heat over medium-high heat. Transfer the chicken to the pan (discarding the marinade) and grill until cooked through, about 12 minutes per side. Remove from the heat and let rest for 10 minutes. Chop the chicken, add it to the salad, and mix gently.

Place a corn husk on each of twelve serving plates. Divide the salad among the corn husks and serve.

PROSCIUTTO, ZUCCHINI, and GOAT CHEESE FRITTATA

SERVES 6 TO 8

2 tablespoons olive oil

2 large shallots, thinly sliced

6 ounces thinly sliced prosciutto, coarsely chopped

1 large zucchini, coarsely chopped

Kosher salt and freshly ground black pepper

8 large eggs

½ cup heavy cream

1 cup Monterey Jack cheese, or any other melting cheese

1 cup crumbled goat cheese

A good frittata recipe is clutch in your entertaining repertoire. It's super easy to make, can be prepared ahead of time, and sits well at room temperature. This one gets salty pops of flavor from the prosciutto and goat cheese, which are terrific with a mild veg, like zucchini. I love this frittata for brunch, or for lunch with a peppery arugula salad. If you ask me, I'd also serve some hot sauce or chipotles in adobo on the side for a little kick!

Preheat the oven to 350°F.

Heat the olive oil in a heavy oven-safe 8-inch skillet over medium heat. Add the shallots and cook, stirring, until translucent, about 6 minutes. Add the prosciutto and cook, stirring occasionally, until it is slightly crispy, about 10 minutes. Add the zucchini and cook, stirring, until softened, about 6 minutes more. Season to taste with salt and pepper, spread the mixture in an even layer in the skillet, and remove from the heat.

Beat the eggs and cream in a large bowl. Fold both cheeses into the egg mixture, then pour the mixture into the skillet. Cook over medium heat until the frittata is just set at the edges, about 10 minutes. Transfer the skillet to the oven and bake until the frittata is set, about 20 minutes. Run a knife around the frittata to loosen it, then slide it out onto a platter. Let cool for 30 minutes, then slice into wedges and serve.

MINI CRAB CAKES with HABANERO MAYO

MAKES 28 CRAB CAKES (SERVES 12 TO 14)

1 pound lump crabmeat, picked over to remove any shell, broken into small pieces

1½ cups panko bread crumbs

¼ cup plus 2 tablespoons mayonnaise

1 large egg, beaten

½ cup chopped fresh cilantro leaves

¼ cup chopped scallions (white and pale green parts only)

1 tablespoon freshly squeezed lime juice

1 teaspoon hot sauce, such as Tabasco

Kosher salt and freshly ground black pepper

1 tablespoon Dijon mustard

2 teaspoons habanero hot sauce

1 teaspoon honey

¼ cup olive oil

Chopped fresh chives, for garnish

Serve crab cakes at a gathering, and your guests instantly feel special. Just be sure to use very high-quality crabmeat, which is now available at many markets. If you have a good fishmonger who can get you fresh, sweet crab legs, all the better! What I will never use in my entire life is imitation crabmeat. I mean, make a meatball instead and forgo the crab cake altogether. I want the true star of this dish to be the actual crab, so I don't add a ton of filler. You can totally prep the cakes in advance and freeze them to minimize your stress the day of the party.

Combine the crab, ½ cup of the panko, 2 tablespoons of the mayonnaise, the egg, cilantro, scallions, lime juice, and hot sauce in a medium bowl. Mix until the ingredients are combined. Season to taste with salt and pepper. Form the mixture into small patties, about 1 tablespoon each, and place them on a platter. Cover and refrigerate for about 20 minutes.

Combine the remaining ¼ cup mayonnaise, the mustard, habanero sauce, and honey in a small bowl. Season to taste with salt and pepper. Set aside.

Place the remaining 1 cup panko on a plate. Coat the crab patties on both sides with the panko.

Heat the olive oil in a large nonstick skillet over medium-high heat. Add the crab cakes in batches and cook for 2 to 3 minutes on each side, until golden and crisp on the outside. Transfer the crab cakes to a platter, dollop each with the habanero mayo, sprinkle with chives, and serve.

SALSA de MOLCAJETE

MAKES ABOUT 2 CUPS

3 large tomatoes

2 chiles de árbol

2 garlic cloves, unpeeled

1 jalapeño

1 teaspoon kosher salt, plus more to taste

½ medium white onion, coarsely chopped

Juice of 1 lemon

Extra-virgin olive oil, for drizzling

If I had a nickel for every time Philip said, "We need to sell this salsa so we can retire," I actually *could* retire right now. I make this salsa the traditional way—pounded in a *molcajete*, Mexico's version of a mortar and pestle made from volcanic rock. What's not traditional is adding olive oil and serving the salsa warm. Also not typical is the lemon, which adds a tart but sweet kick. But what really makes the salsa so good is blackening the veggies all over. Just char the heck out of everything in a completely dry pan. However, take care not to burst the tomatoes, because then the juices will run out and you won't get a char. I like to serve the salsa dolloped alongside meats and fish or as an addictive dip for tortilla chips. The salsa works with pretty much everything—I've even caught Philip and some guests eating it by the spoonful!

Dry-roast the tomatoes, chiles de árbol, garlic, and jalapeño in a cast-iron skillet over medium-high heat. When the garlic's papery outer skin starts to brown, remove the garlic from the pan and carefully peel it, discarding the skin. Cook the tomatoes, chile de árbol, and jalapeño until soft and blackened on all sides, taking care to keep the tomato skins intact. Transfer to a plate to cool. Peel and stem the jalapeño.

Place the garlic in a molcajete and season with the salt. Grind with the pestle until a paste forms. Add the chiles de árbol and grind until they break into tiny pieces. Repeat with the jalapeño. Add the tomatoes, one at a time, and grind until smooth. Add the onion and grind until incorporated. Add the lemon juice and stir to combine. Drizzle the salsa with olive oil, season generously with salt, and serve immediately while still warm.

tres: SWEETS

ZUCCHINI BREAD

**MAKES ONE
9 X 5-INCH LOAF**

4 tablespoons (½ stick) unsalted butter, melted, plus more at room temperature

1½ cups all-purpose flour, plus more for dusting

1½ cups grated summer squash (I use a mix of yellow squash and zucchini)

1 cup granulated sugar

¼ cup vegetable oil

2 large eggs

2 teaspoons ground cinnamon

2 teaspoons pure vanilla extract

½ teaspoon kosher salt

½ teaspoon baking soda

½ teaspoon baking powder

This zucchini bread is my son David's favorite thing in the world to eat. But that doesn't mean you, as an adult, won't absolutely love it. If you're like me, entertaining usually means inviting entire families—I actually prefer that when throwing parties. The parents are always grateful to have an option that'll appeal to the littles, and this one's packed with veggies, to boot. A win-win in my book! This bread is a delicious multitasker for gatherings: I set the loaf on the table with soft butter to accompany the meal or to nibble on beforehand. It also makes for a no-fuss, not-too-sweet dessert. So eat your veggies, or, even better, your zucchini bread!

Preheat the oven to 350°F. Grease a 9 x 5-inch loaf pan generously with butter, then coat lightly with flour and tap out any excess.

Combine the melted butter, flour, zucchini, sugar, vegetable oil, eggs, cinnamon, vanilla salt, baking soda, and baking powder in a large bowl and mix with a wooden spoon until the batter is well blended and the zucchini is evenly distributed. Pour the batter into the prepared pan and bake until a tester inserted into the center comes out clean, about 45 minutes. Remove from the oven and let the loaf cool in the pan on a wire rack for 15 minutes before turning it out. Slice and serve warm, with plenty of softened butter!

POUND CAKE with POACHED PEARS and CAJETA

SERVES 6

2 cups dry red wine, such as Cabernet Sauvignon

¼ cup orange juice

2 tablespoons light brown sugar

1 cinnamon stick

½ teaspoon ground cardamom

3 small firm but ripe Bosc pears, peeled, halved, and cored

1 cup cajeta (goat's-milk caramel) or dulce de leche

1 (1-pound) butter pound cake

½ cup finely chopped pecans

Show up to a party with this showstopper dessert, and I guarantee your friends will think you spent three days making it. But (*shhh*) it's made with store-bought pound cake that's filled with elegant poached pears, then drizzled with a delectable red wine–caramel sauce. It's good to keep these types of shortcuts in your back pocket, because we all deserve a little break when entertaining. I almost feel guilty for presenting something so stunning with so little work. Almost.

Combine the red wine, orange juice, brown sugar, cinnamon stick, and cardamom in a medium pot and bring to a boil, stirring occasionally to make sure the sugar completely dissolves. Add the pears, reduce the heat to medium-low, and simmer until the pears are tender, turning occasionally, 12 to 15 minutes. Using a slotted spoon, transfer the pears to a medium bowl. Bring the poaching liquid to a boil and cook until reduced to ½ cup, about 15 minutes. Add the cajeta and stir until combined. Remove from the heat.

Using a knife, carve out a trench from the center of the pound cake, leaving a ½-inch border all around and making sure not to cut all the way through the cake. Set aside until ready to assemble.

Stand the poached pears upright in the trench of the cake, drizzle with the cajeta syrup, then sprinkle with the chopped pecans and serve right away.

COCONUT-LIME CHEESECAKE BITES

MAKES 16 MINI SQUARES

Nonstick cooking spray

1 (4-ounce) sleeve graham crackers (9 crackers)

6 tablespoons (¾ stick) unsalted butter, melted and cooled

1 tablespoon granulated sugar, plus more for sprinkling

1½ cups unsweetened shredded coconut, toasted

2 (8-ounce) packages cream cheese, at room temperature

1 (14-ounce) can sweetened condensed milk

1 tablespoon grated lime zest, plus more for sprinkling

¼ cup freshly squeezed lime juice

1 teaspoon pure vanilla extract

1 lime, sliced into 16 thin wedges

This luscious dessert is an all-star MVP for parties. You can assemble it ahead, chill it in the fridge, then serve it the next day. I slice the cheesecake into little squares and set them out on a table with other desserts so guests can help themselves to a few different sweets. This also means you won't have to pry yourself away from that great conversation and miss out!

———

Preheat the oven to 350°F. Spray an 8½-inch square baking pan with cooking spray and line it with parchment paper, leaving a 2-inch overhang on each side.

Combine the graham crackers, butter, and sugar in a food processor and process until moist crumbs form. Add ½ cup of the toasted coconut and stir with a rubber spatula to combine (do not process in the food processor).

Transfer the crumb mixture to the prepared baking pan and press it over the bottom and 1 inch up the sides. Bake the crust until golden brown, about 12 minutes. Remove from the oven and let cool.

Meanwhile, using a handheld mixer, beat the cream cheese in a large bowl on high speed until smooth. Beat in the condensed milk a little at a time, scraping the sides of the bowl as necessary. Add the lime zest, lime juice, and vanilla and beat until well combined.

Pour the filling into the cooled crust and smooth the top with a rubber spatula. Cover with plastic wrap and refrigerate until firm, 2½ to 3 hours.

Use the overhanging parchment to lift the cheesecake out of the pan and set it on a cutting board. Sprinkle the remaining 1 cup toasted coconut over the cheesecake, cut it into 16 squares, and arrange them on a platter. Top each square with a lime wedge and sprinkle each lime with sugar and lime zest. Chill until ready to serve, up to 3 hours. Serve chilled.

MANGO WHIPPED CREAM BERRY TRIFLES

SERVES 4

1 ripe mango, peeled and cut into small pieces

1 cup plus 2 tablespoons granulated sugar

2 tablespoons freshly squeezed lime juice

1 cup heavy cream

5 cups cubed pound cake (from one 1-pound store-bought loaf)

½ cup sweetened condensed milk

2 cups sliced strawberries

1 cup blueberries

4 fresh mint leaves, for garnish

SPECIAL EQUIPMENT:

4 (16-ounce) mason jars

Individual desserts in mason jars are not just fun and cute—they're easy to store and serve. This recipe for simple mason jar trifles comes together in minutes and still looks super Pinterest-y on your dessert table. The trifles are layered with a whipped cream mixed with pureed mango. Be sure the mango is ripe enough that it's sweet. Otherwise, you could use canned. Just drain the mango well so your cream isn't too runny.

Combine the mango, 2 tablespoons of the sugar, and the lime juice in a food processor or blender. Process until smooth. Combine the cream and remaining 1 cup sugar in a stand mixer fitted with the whisk attachment. Whisk on high until stiff peaks form, 2 minutes. Add the mango puree and whisk on medium until the ingredients are combined. Do not overbeat the whipped cream. Cover and refrigerate until ready to assemble the trifles.

Put about ½ cup of the pound cake cubes in each jar. Drizzle 1 tablespoon of the sweetened condensed milk over the pound cake in each jar. Add half the strawberries and blueberries to the jars. Top the berries with half the mango whipped cream, or enough to cover the berries. Divide the remaining pound cake among the jars, followed by the remaining condensed milk, mango whipped cream, and berries. Cover the jars and refrigerate for about 1 hour before serving. Top each trifle with a mint leaf and serve.

MOSTACHON
(STRAWBERRY MERINGUE CAKE)

SERVES 10

CAKE

Nonstick cooking spray

4 large egg whites

1 cup granulated sugar

1 teaspoon pure vanilla extract

½ teaspoon baking powder

Pinch of kosher salt

1 cup chopped walnuts

1 (15.8-ounce) package Maria crackers, chopped

FROSTING

1 (8-ounce) package cream cheese, at room temperature

½ cup sour cream

½ cup powdered sugar

1 teaspoon pure vanilla extract

1½ pounds fresh strawberries, sliced, for garnish

This cake is said to have been created in Monterrey, Mexico, but was surely inspired by *marjolaine* or any of the meringue-based desserts brought over to us by the French. While the French like to mix nuts into their meringues, someone in this northern Mexican town came up with the brilliant idea to also add *galletas marias*—Mexico's version of a tea biscuit. The resulting cake is soft, chewy, and crunchy, all at the same time. You cover it with a luxurious cream cheese frosting, then decorate the top with sliced strawberries. It's sure to be a superstar at your next dessert table!

FOR THE CAKE, preheat the oven to 350°F. Spray a 9-inch springform pan with cooking spray.

Put the egg whites in the bowl of a stand mixer fitted with the whisk attachment. Beat on high speed until soft peaks form. With the mixer running, slowly add the granulated sugar, then the vanilla, baking powder, and salt and beat for about 2 minutes. Turn the power off and fold in the walnuts and Maria crackers with a rubber spatula. Transfer to the prepared pan. Bake for 30 to 35 minutes, until golden brown. Let cool in the pan on a wire rack for 15 minutes.

recipe continues

MEANWHILE, FOR THE FROSTING, combine the cream cheese, sour cream, powdered sugar, and vanilla extract in the bowl of a stand mixer fitted with the whisk attachment. Beat on medium-high speed until soft peaks form and the mixture is smooth.

TO ASSEMBLE, release the sides of the springform pan and transfer the cake to a platter. Using an offset spatula, spread the frosting all over the cake. Arrange the strawberries in a concentric pattern on top of the cake, slice into wedges, and serve.

DULCE de LECHE CREAM PUFFS

MAKES 24 CREAM PUFFS

Pâte à Choux (see page 148)

DULCE DE LECHE WHIPPED CREAM

2 cups heavy cream

1 cup dulce de leche

Cream puffs are one of those pastries that sound intimidating to make, but they're actually quite simple. You basically pipe out the dough (called pâte à choux) into mounds, bake them into crispy shells, then fill them with whatever you like. Here I went Lat-Am with a dulce de leche whipped cream that melts in your mouth with each bite of cream puff pillow.

Prepare the pâte à choux dough and transfer it to a pastry bag fitted with a large tip. Pipe about twenty-four 2-inch mounds on the prepared baking sheet. Bake for 20 to 25 minutes, until the pastry shells are golden brown on top.

Meanwhile, for the dulce de leche whipped cream, place the cream in the bowl of a stand mixer fitted with the whisk attachment. Beat on medium speed for about 3 minutes, until soft peaks form. Using a rubber spatula, fold in the dulce de leche until just combined.

Remove the pastry shells from the oven, pierce each shell with a toothpick, and let cool completely. Transfer the dulce de leche whipped cream to a pastry bag fitted with a medium tip. Pipe the cream into the cooled pastry shells, transfer to a platter, and serve immediately.

ATE CON QUESO
(QUINCE PASTE WITH CHEESE) ON A SALT BOARD

SERVES 6

1 (4-ounce) wedge Manchego cheese

4 ounces ate de membrillo (quince paste)

Edible flowers, for garnish (optional)

SPECIAL EQUIPMENT:

8 x 12-inch Himalayan salt block (available at specialty markets and from Amazon)

I always have *ate* (fruit paste, pronounced "*ah-tay*") in my pantry because it pretty much lasts forever. Quince paste, in particular, is fabulous with cheese. This is seriously my go-to appetizer for impromptu get-togethers. My fiancé, Philip, is in charge of making sure we always have at least one chunk of good cheese to pair with the *ate*. While it's a very traditional pairing in all of Latin America, the sweet fruit with earthy, creamy cheese appeals to everyone at a party. Serving on a salt block not only makes for a stunning presentation, but also imparts great flavor to the cheese.

Slice the cheese into ¼-inch-thick wedges, discarding the rind. Slice the quince paste into ⅛-inch-thick rectangles. Top the cheese wedges with the quince paste slices, arrange on the salt board, garnish with flowers, and serve.

MINI GUAVA FLANS with SALTED CARAMEL

MAKES 11 INDIVIDUAL FLANS

FLANS

Nonstick cooking spray

1 (14-ounce) can sweetened condensed milk

1 (12-ounce) can evaporated milk

1 (8-ounce) package cream cheese, at room temperature

5 large eggs

¾ cup guava fruit spread

2 teaspoons pure vanilla extract

Pinch of salt

CARAMEL

1 cup packed light brown sugar

4 tablespoons (½ cup) unsalted butter

2 tablespoons water

Coarse sea salt, for garnish

SPECIAL EQUIPMENT:

11 (½-cup/4-ounce) oven-safe jars

You won't find a dessert that's easier to prep than these upside-down flans with caramel on top. You basically combine the ingredients in a blender and push a button. What I love even more about this version is that the flan is baked individually in the jars they'll be served in. No need to worry about slicing it up and breaking out the dessert plates. The guava fruit spread brings a beautiful flavor that's reminiscent of strawberry and pear. It's absolutely delicious mellowed out by the creaminess of the flan base.

FOR THE FLANS, preheat the oven to 325°F. Spray the jars with cooking spray.

Combine the condensed milk, evaporated milk, cream cheese, eggs, guava spread, vanilla, and salt in a blender. Blend until smooth. Divide the mixture among the prepared jars. Transfer the jars to a large roasting pan. Fill the pan with enough water to come halfway up the sides of the jars. Cover the entire pan with aluminum foil. Bake until the centers of the flans jiggle slightly when moved, about 25 minutes. Carefully remove the jars from the pan and let cool for 30 minutes. Cover and refrigerate for at least 3 hours or up to overnight.

FOR THE CARAMEL, combine the brown sugar, butter, and water in a medium saucepan over medium heat. Bring to a boil, stirring continuously, then reduce the heat to low and simmer until an amber caramel forms, about 2 minutes. Remove from the heat and let cool.

Divide the cooled caramel among the jars of flan, top each with a sprinkle of sea salt, and serve.

TIRAMISU

SERVES 10 TO 12

3 large eggs, separated

3 tablespoons granulated sugar

8 ounces mascarpone cheese

2 cups brewed coffee, cooled

10 ounces ladyfingers

1 cup shaved dark chocolate, plus more for garnish

I don't drink coffee, but I will happily get my after-dinner caffeine buzz from this creamy, rich tiramisu. And guess what? You can prep it right in a container that goes from the fridge to the table. My sister-in-law Lisa actually passed this recipe to my mom's best friend and my neighbor, Ms. Encinas, who then passed it down to her daughter Elizabeth, who is now *my* neighbor. It would have been easier to get the recipe directly from Lisa, but this way a whole bunch of people I love a lot got a chance to taste this dessert.

———

Using a handheld mixer, beat the egg yolks and sugar in a large metal bowl on high speed until pale, 5 to 8 minutes. Beat in the mascarpone until just combined. Set aside.

Clean the mixer beaters very well and dry them. Using the mixer, beat the egg whites in a separate large bowl on high speed until soft peaks form. Using a rubber spatula, fold the egg whites into the mascarpone mixture and set aside.

Pour the coffee into a shallow bowl. Dip both sides of half the ladyfingers into the coffee, lining them up over the bottom of a 9 x 13-inch baking pan in three rows and trimming the edges to fit, if necessary, as you go. Evenly spread half the mascarpone mixture on top. Repeat with the remaining ladyfingers and mascarpone mixture. Sprinkle the shaved chocolate over the mascarpone mixture. Cover and refrigerate the tiramisu for at least 6 hours and up to overnight.

Let the tiramisu stand at room temperature for 30 minutes before serving. Garnish with more shaved chocolate, cut into squares, and serve.

ULTIMATE CHOCOLATE CAKE

MAKES ONE 9-INCH LAYER CAKE (SERVES 10 TO 12)

CAKE

Nonstick cooking spray

2 cups all-purpose flour

2 cups granulated sugar

¾ cup unsweetened cocoa powder

2 teaspoons baking soda

1 teaspoon baking powder

1 teaspoon kosher salt

1 cup whole milk

1 cup boiling water

½ cup vegetable oil

2 large eggs

1 tablespoon pure vanilla extract

FROSTING

1¾ cups powdered sugar

3 tablespoons unsalted butter, at room temperature

4½ ounces bittersweet chocolate, melted

½ cup sour cream

Moist, rich, and decadent, this is the chocolate cake of your dreams. My dear pastry chef friend Elsa Flores developed the recipe for me to demo on *The Kitchen*. I love the bit of tang the cake gets from sour cream. It reminds me of my mother's desserts (she managed to sneak sour cream into a lot of sweets). Bring this layer cake out at a party and watch as people's faces light up.

FOR THE CAKE, preheat the oven to 350°F. Spray two 9-inch round cake pans with cooking spray.

Combine the flour, granulated sugar, cocoa powder, baking soda, baking powder, and salt in the bowl of a stand mixer fitted with the paddle attachment. Mix on low speed until well combined. With the mixer on low speed, add the milk, boiling water, vegetable oil, eggs, and vanilla. Mix on high speed for 1 minute, scraping down the sides as needed, until the mixture is well combined and has air bubbles forming on the top.

Divide the batter between the prepared pans and bake until a cake tester inserted into the center of each comes out clean, about 40 minutes. Remove from the oven and let cool in the pans on wire racks for about 10 minutes. Run a thin knife around the edge of each cake, then invert them onto the racks and let cool completely, 20 to 30 minutes.

MEANWHILE, FOR THE FROSTING, combine the powdered sugar and butter in a food processor and pulse until well combined. Add the melted chocolate and pulse, scraping down the sides as needed, until the chocolate is fully incorporated. Add the sour cream and process until very smooth, about 1 minute.

Flip the cakes right-side up and, using a serrated knife, gently trim off the domed top of each cake layer to completely level it. (Save the trimmings for another use.) Place one cake layer on a platter and spread half the frosting on top. Top with the second cake layer, trimmed-side down. Spread the remaining frosting only on the top of the cake, leaving the sides uncovered. Cut into wedges and serve.

COCONUT MACAROONS DRIZZLED with DARK CHOCOLATE

Nonstick cooking spray

1 (14-ounce) bag sweetened shredded coconut (about 5½ cups)

½ cup sweetened condensed milk

2 cups semisweet chocolate chips, melted and cooled slightly

I can make three dozen of these cookies for a gathering, and they always disappear. I mean, what's not to love? Chewy morsels of coconut and sweetened condensed milk topped with chocolate. They also happen to be gluten-free. If you want to get creative, drizzle some melted white chocolate over the finished macaroons. It's super easy but will make you look like a fancy pastry chef.

Preheat the oven to 350°F. Spray a baking sheet with cooking spray.

Mix the coconut and condensed milk in a large bowl until well combined. Drop mounds (about 1 tablespoon each) onto the prepared baking sheet.

Bake until the coconut is golden brown with crispy edges, about 20 minutes. Remove from the oven and let cool slightly. Dip a fork into the chocolate and drizzle it over the macaroons. Refrigerate on the baking sheet until the chocolate is firm, about 30 minutes, then transfer to a platter and serve.

WHITE CHOCOLATE and APRICOT OATMEAL COOKIES

MAKES ABOUT 24 COOKIES

1 cup (2 sticks) unsalted butter, at room temperature

1 cup packed light brown sugar

1 cup granulated sugar

2 large eggs, at room temperature

2 teaspoons pure vanilla extract

1½ cups all-purpose flour

1 teaspoon baking powder

1 teaspoon ground cinnamon

1 teaspoon kosher salt

3 cups old-fashioned oats

1 cup dried apricots, coarsely chopped

¾ cup white chocolate chips

Nonstick cooking spray

The inspiration for this recipe is my mom, who loved to dip dried apricots in white chocolate for a snack. I turn that combo into these next-level oatmeal cookies. The dough spreads a bit as it bakes, but that's a very good thing! You end up with crispy edges on the cookies that taste of nutty brown butter. Meanwhile, the centers are chewy-soft with sweet-and-tangy dried apricots. My guests are absolutely delighted when I serve these cookies with coffee after a meal.

Combine the butter, brown sugar, and granulated sugar in the bowl of a stand mixer fitted with the paddle attachment. Beat on medium-high speed until light and fluffy, about 2 minutes. With the mixer on low, add the eggs, one at a time. Add the vanilla and beat for 1 minute more.

In a separate bowl, sift together the flour, baking powder, cinnamon, and salt. With the mixer on low, slowly add the dry ingredients to the wet ingredients and mix until combined. Using a rubber spatula, fold in the oats, apricots, and white chocolate chips, making sure everything is evenly incorporated. Cover the bowl with plastic wrap and refrigerate for 1 hour before baking.

Preheat the oven to 325°F. Spray two baking sheets with cooking spray.

Using a 4-ounce ice cream scoop, drop 2-inch mounds of the dough onto the prepared baking sheets about 1 inch apart. Bake until golden in color, 14 to 16 minutes. Transfer the cookies to a wire rack and let cool completely, then transfer to a platter and serve.

PAVLOVAS with CITRUS CURD and BLACKBERRIES

MAKES ABOUT 20 PAVLOVAS

CITRUS CURD

¼ cup freshly squeezed lemon juice (from about 1½ lemons)

¼ cup freshly squeezed blood orange or other orange juice (from about 1 orange)

1 teaspoon grated lemon zest, plus more for sprinkling

1 teaspoon grated blood orange or other orange zest, plus more for sprinkling

½ cup granulated sugar

3 large eggs

6 tablespoons (¾ stick) unsalted butter, cut into pieces

PAVLOVAS

4 large egg whites

1¼ cups granulated sugar

2 teaspoons cornstarch, sifted

1 teaspoon pure vanilla extract

1 teaspoon freshly squeezed lemon juice

12 ounces blackberries

Fresh mint leaves, for garnish

Pavlovas are named after the Russian ballet dancer Anna Pavlova. And like the ballerina (as well as my own daughter, Anna), these little meringue desserts are delicate and beautiful. Achieving the perfect pavlova is all about timing and temperature. Bake the meringues low and slow so they're wonderfully crisp on the outside and soft on the inside. You don't want to end up with crunchy pavlovas that are hard all the way through. The citrus curd nestled in the center of the meringues is made with blood orange juice, which gives the dish a lovely sunset color and fantastic flavor.

FOR THE CITRUS CURD, whisk together the citrus juices, zests, granulated sugar, and eggs in a small saucepan. Set the pan over low heat and stir in the butter. Cook, whisking frequently, until the curd has thickened, 5 to 6 minutes.

Transfer the citrus curd to a small bowl and let cool. Cover with plastic wrap and refrigerate until set, at least 1 hour and up to 1 day.

FOR THE PAVLOVAS, preheat the oven to 250°F. Line two baking sheets with parchment paper.

Using a handheld mixer, beat the egg whites in a large bowl on high speed until soft peaks form. Gradually beat in the granulated sugar and beat until stiff peaks form. Using a rubber spatula, gently fold the cornstarch, vanilla, and lemon juice just until incorporated.

Spoon the meringue onto the prepared baking sheets in 20 mounds (about 2 tablespoons each), spacing them apart. Using the back of a spoon, make an indentation in the center of each mound to create a nest. Bake the meringues until crisp and barely golden on the outside but still soft on the inside, about 50 minutes. Using a metal spatula, transfer the meringues to a wire rack and let cool completely. (If not assembling the pavlovas immediately, store the cooled meringues in a single layer in an airtight container at room temperature for up to 1 day.)

TO ASSEMBLE, divide the citrus curd filling evenly among the meringues. Top with the blackberries, mint leaves, citrus zests, transfer to a platter, and serve.

STICKY DATE MINI BUNDTS

MAKES 6 MINI CAKES

CAKE

Nonstick cooking spray

1¼ cups chopped pitted dates

1¼ cups water

1 teaspoon baking soda

1½ cups all-purpose flour

1 teaspoon baking powder

¼ teaspoon ground cinnamon

¼ teaspoon kosher salt

4 tablespoons (½ stick) unsalted butter, at room temperature

1 cup granulated sugar

2 large eggs

2 teaspoons pure vanilla extract

––––––

PILONCILLO SAUCE

1½ cups finely minced piloncillo (unrefined whole cane sugar; available at Latin markets)

½ cup (1 stick) unsalted butter, cubed

½ cup heavy cream

1 teaspoon pure vanilla extract

––––––

½ teaspoon kosher salt

Vanilla ice cream, for serving

––––––

SPECIAL EQUIPMENT:

6 mini Bundt pans

––––––

Not to brag, but this dessert never fails to get cries of "OMG" or "Wow!" at my parties. Guests go crazy for this take on the UK dessert that I bake in mini Bundt pans. It's called sticky toffee pudding across the pond, but it's actually a cake, and it's sticky from chopped dates and a good soak in toffee sauce. The trick to keeping these little cakes super moist is poking them all over with a skewer when they are fresh out of the oven, then drizzling them with warm syrup. I make my syrup with piloncillo, a type of dark sugar that's common in Mexico, which gives the syrup a deep, complex flavor. Serving the cake with vanilla ice cream is not optional. When the ice cream melts, it's like a crème anglaise sauce and seeps into the porous, sticky cake.

FOR THE CAKE, preheat the oven to 350°F. Spray the Bundt pans generously with cooking spray.

Combine the dates and water in a medium saucepan and bring to a boil. Remove from the heat, stir in the baking soda, and let cool.

In a medium bowl, sift together the flour, baking powder, cinnamon, and salt. Combine the butter and granulated sugar in the bowl of a stand mixer fitted with the paddle attachment. Beat on medium speed until light and fluffy, 1 to 2 minutes. Beat in the eggs and vanilla. In two alternating batches, beat in the dry ingredients and the date mixture until just incorporated. Divide the batter between the prepared pans and bake for 20 minutes, or until a tester inserted into the center of each comes out clean. Remove from the oven and let the cakes cool in the pans on wire racks for 10 minutes.

MEANWHILE, FOR THE PILONCILLO SAUCE, combine the piloncillo, butter, and cream in a medium saucepan. Bring to a boil over medium heat, whisking to dissolve the sugar. Reduce the heat to medium-low and simmer, whisking continuously, for 2 minutes. Remove from the heat. Whisk in the vanilla and salt. Keep the sauce warm.

Using a skewer, poke holes all over the warm cakes and pour half the piloncillo sauce over. Let stand until the cakes have absorbed the syrup. Turn the cakes out onto a platter and pour the remaining sauce over them. Serve warm with vanilla ice cream.

PALETAS DE FRESAS CON CREMA
(STRAWBERRIES-AND-CREAM ICE POPS)

MAKES 10 ICE POPS

1 pound fresh strawberries, hulled and sliced

1 (14-ounce) can sweetened condensed milk

1 cup whole milk

SPECIAL EQUIPMENT:

10 ice pop molds, 10 ice pop sticks

In Mexico, *paletas* are fresh fruit ice pops. When I was a kid, walking into the *paleteria* and getting my strawberries-and-cream *paleta* was the ultimate reward at the end of a tiring school week. Paletas can be either milk- or juice-based. I usually prefer the latter, but when it comes to strawberries, creamy is the way to go. I love to serve these at parties, where they bring a smile to everyone's faces.

Combine the strawberries and condensed milk in a medium bowl and mash with a wooden spoon. Alternatively, leave the strawberry slices intact instead of mashing them. Add the whole milk and stir until well combined.

Divide the mixture evenly among the ice pop molds. Insert the ice pop sticks, cover the molds, and freeze overnight or for up to 1 week. Unmold the ice pops and serve right away.

index

Page numbers in *italics*
indicate illustrations.